Standing Out

My Look, My Style, My Life

Standing Out

My Look, My Style, My Life

Katie Price

CENTURY

Published by Century 2009

2 4 6 8 10 9 7 5 3 1

First published in Great Britain in 2009 by
Century
Random House, 20 Vauxhall Bridge Road,
London SW1V 2SA

www.randomhouse.co.uk

Addresses for companies within The Random House Group Limited can be found at: www.randomhouse.co.uk

The Random House Group Limited Reg. No. 954009

A CIP catalogue record for this book
is available from the British Library

ISBN 9781846056680

The Random House Group Limited supports The Forest Stewardship
Council (FSC), the leading international forest certification organisation. All our
titles that are printed on Greenpeace approved FSC certified paper carry the FSC logo. Our paper procurement policy
can be found at www.rbooks.co.uk/environment

Printed and bound in Germany by
Firmengruppe APPL, Aprinta Druck, Wemding

Design by www.envydesign.co.uk

CONTENTS

INTRODUCTION

I know what some people will be thinking: Katie Price writing a style book? You're having a laugh! Since becoming famous I've often been slated for the way I dress just because I've never followed fashion or worn the sort of outfits you see in the glossy mags. I don't care what people say – everyone's entitled to their own opinion. But to me, looking good is more about confidence and attitude rather than wearing the latest designer label. Besides, I would far rather be slagged off for being a bit outrageous and having fun with my look than turn up on the red carpet in exactly the same dress as someone else.

Although I do work with stylists on photo shoots and occasionally for big events, I can safely say that unlike most celebrities my style is 100 per cent my own – and it's a style that hasn't changed since I was an 18-year-old model living in Brighton, dreaming of stardom. When I first became famous it was almost as much for the outfits I wore as what I got up to while I was wearing them. In those early years most people knew me as Jordan, the outrageous bad girl who liked her skirts short, her heels sky-high and her make-up piled on with a JCB. These days I'm more likely to be caught on camera in a girlie tracksuit and flip-flops (only because with kids and a career I don't have so many opportunities to get my outrageous dresses out!) but my look has played a central role in getting me where I am today.

I'm not writing this book to tell the nation how to get dressed. If you want to know what style of jeans best suits a pear-shaped bum or whether horizontal stripes make you look fat, you're not going to find it in these pages; I'm all about individuality and making the most of your own look. But over the years I've had so many questions from fans about my style that I wanted to share the secrets of how I put my look together, from the places I shop to my make-up essentials.

As you'll see, what I wear changes according to the different roles I play in my life – I'm starting a new life as an independent working mum, I'm a businesswoman, a celebrity and of course I'm Jordan – but whatever I'm doing and however I'm dressed, I always like to make sure that I'm Standing Out.

My Look, My Way

This is me. It's not often that anyone other than close friends and my family see me stripped back to basics like this – gone are the big hair and make-up, the high heels and hot pants. This is what I see in the mirror every morning after I've got out of the bath and before I get ready to face the world. When it comes to styling yourself, I think it's really important for every girl to strip off and take a long, hard look at herself from all angles in a full-length mirror so that she can see what she's got to work with. It's what I like to call the bare necessities. You need to recognise your best features so you can show them off, and it's good to be aware of the not-so-good bits which might need a bit of covering up. For instance, I love my green eyes but I'm not so keen on my knobbly knees or my finger, which looks like a Nik Nak after I had an operation to remove a cancerous growth in 2002, or the fact that my belly pops out and I end up looking pregnant every time I eat anything. It's important to be completely honest with yourself.

So are you ready? Right, let's get dressed...

From an early age I've always worn whatever I wanted

THE EARLY YEARS

'Oh my god, Kate, what have you got on?' Mum was standing at the bottom of the stairs, staring in horror at the tiny black PVC dress I was wearing. I gave her a little twirl and smiled broadly. It was exactly the reaction I wanted.

It was the day of my stepdad Paul's 40th birthday and I must have been about 13. As it was a special occasion, Mum had given me some money the week before so I could buy a new outfit for the party. Going shopping was a bit of a novelty for me at the time, as most of the clothes in my wardrobe were

hand-me-downs from my mum's friend who had a daughter a bit older than me or jumpers and cardigans that Mum had knitted herself. Not that I minded much – I was so into my horses that the little pocket money I did have went on them, and I spent most of the time in jodhpurs and boots anyway. I was much happier in jodhpurs as I was painfully self-conscious about my skinny legs; so much so that if I had to wear a skirt I'd put on two pairs of leggings to try and fatten them up. But from my early teens I began to have this urge to stand out from the crowd. I became obsessed with catsuits and would daydream about being this sexy girl with big boobs who drove a black Suzuki Vitara jeep wearing a slinky black velvet catsuit and high heels. God knows where I got that idea from, as I was this skinny little thing and the posters on my bedroom wall were of horses, not pop stars. But I was convinced that was the girl I wanted to be when I grew up. So when Mum told me I could choose a new outfit to wear for my stepdad's party, I knew exactly the sort of thing I wanted, and I found it in Topshop – short, black, shiny and very sexy. With the help of loads of shoulder pads stuffed down my bra, I thought I looked amazing. In the end Mum just rolled her eyes and let me wear it; even then she knew that once I set my mind to something, there's no point trying to talk me out of it. She still rolls her eyes at some of my outfit choices today!

I've always been an exhibitionist. Although I was never into slavishly following fashion, by the time I turned 15 I was desperate to look different from the other girls in my school so I'd mess with my uniform to try and funk it up a bit. I'd do my make-up on the bus, as my stepdad hated me wearing it. I wasn't from a particularly well-off family, so I was never the girl with the latest trainers or the must-have bag, but I wasn't the one who got picked on for having the wrong shoes either ('Molly' shoes, I call them, a word we use in Brighton to describe anything that makes someone look frumpy and older than they are). But even back then I had my own unique style. I remember one year chunky platform boots were in, so I customised mine by sticking loads of drawing pins in a pattern on the soles.

We had a uniform at school, but I would always try to make myself stand out. At the start of one year I had a vision of myself in a long, flowing, grey skirt with a white shirt and mac, as if I was this mysterious, sophisticated lady. Weird, eh? If I'd known then what I know now I'd have gone to school dressed like Britney Spears as a slutty schoolgirl in the 'Hit Me, Baby…' video! But whenever I got dressed, I would always have an image in my head of how I wanted to look – and normal was the last thing it would be. Whatever was considered appropriate to wear, I would always be drawn to the opposite.

I remember buying a black 1950s-style swimsuit with a cream trim from Topshop, which I would wear to muck out the horses with just a pair of wellies and long socks pulled up so they were peeping out over the top. Or I would ride my horse bareback and barefoot wearing a bikini top and hot pants. Not in the least bit suitable for the stable yard, but I certainly stood out.

When I was a bit older I started a part-time Saturday job in a local fabric shop. All my wages still went on looking after my horses, but the job would prove extremely useful in other ways. Mum had already taught me to sew and knit when I was much younger, so I could run up horse blankets on our sewing machine at home, but working in the shop taught me all about different fabrics, how to fix poppers and zips and to customise clothes, skills that would also be invaluable years later when I had Harvey and needed to alter all his clothes to fit.

Now I was really ready go to town on my wardrobe…

I must have been about 16 when I was flicking through the newspaper one day and spotted an advert in the back pages for one of those dodgy catalogues featuring naughty lingerie and sexy PVC stuff. You were meant to be over 18 to get it, but I ordered a copy anyway. I was so excited when it finally arrived – the rubber catsuits, fishnet dresses and leather hot pants were exactly the sort of thing that the fantasy me would wear to cruise around in her jeep! I ordered a couple of black rubber dresses and cut one of them in half to make a sexy little top, then with my idol, Baywatch babe Pamela Anderson as my inspiration, I sliced criss-cross strips all down the front to show off my cleavage and fixed it all with poppers. I'd just got into the clubbing scene and would go most weekends, usually with Mum and my cousins, and so that night I wore my new top with a necklace, tiny black hot pants from a brand called Miss Moneypenny and long black boots. From then on there was no stopping me; my outfits became more and more outrageous – the tighter and skimpier the better. Just like nowadays, I was always pretty casual during the day, usually wearing jeans and a T-shirt or my favourite Knickerbox bikinis to hit the beach. But whenever I was going out I would love to get dressed up and turn heads.

Since those early days in Brighton, my own personal style hasn't really changed that much – except now that I've got money I can be a little more experimental with my look. For instance, instead of having just one pair of Ugg boots, I can afford to get them in every colour and style. And while when I was younger I'd only have a couple of pairs of jeans, which I'd alternate with different tops, nowadays I'll hardly ever wear the same thing twice. It's a perk of my job and I've worked hard to be able to do that, but I hope this book will help you discover that you don't need a celebrity salary to look gorgeous.

Style chameleon in action: from cute and girlie to fierce and sexy

STYLE CHAMELEON

There is no such thing as the 'typical' Katie Price look. What I wear depends on what mood I'm in, where I'm going and what I'll be doing that day. For me, clothes and make-up are a way of bringing out all the different aspects of my personality. I'm a mum, girlie girl, a celebrity, a model and a businesswoman, and my wardrobe tends to reflect all those different sides to me. I can be anything from classy and ladylike, to slutty and sexy, to pure chav; you could say that I'm a bit of a style chameleon really.

I suppose most people think of me as quite an outrageous dresser but if I'm honest most of the time I'm in tracksuits as I just love being comfy. I've got them in every colour and style; they're probably the most well-worn items in my wardrobe. Contrary to popular opinion, I'm most definitely not high

maintenance. I do always like to have my hair, brows and nails nicely groomed, but that's about it. It's only when I'm going somewhere I know I'll be photographed that the make-up and hairpieces go on, and the really skimpy stuff comes out.

Whatever I'm wearing, though, I always like to look young and fun. I'm a true girlie girl; I love anything pink or sparkly – or preferably both. Words like 'bubblegum', 'princess' and 'candy girl' sum up my style perfectly. I don't have any interest in dressing like a typical 30-something; instead, my style icon is Barbie. I've just been out and bought a gorgeous bright pink Louis Vuitton bag and got the matching sun visor,

necklace and scarf too. Pure Barbie doll dressing!

There aren't any celebrities whose style I particularly admire, but I do like the way Paris Hilton puts her outfits together. She actually reminds me of the way I dress, as her clothes and accessories always match perfectly and she looks immaculate, even if she's just in a tracksuit. My taste in clothes has always been very American, very LA starlet. Regardless of the weather, I dress like it is 30 degrees Celsius and bright sunshine outside.

The one style I really can't stand is goth, probably because it's the complete opposite of the girlie look I love. Don't get me wrong – I do have some goth friends and if it's done well it is a style that can suit certain people, but it wouldn't look good on me. Perhaps it's because I never went to university, as most people seem to go through a grungy stage when they're studying, but I like to be fresh and pretty looking. I'm obsessed with being clean and smelling nice.

Malibu Barbie!

One of my early modelling shots. Look at those curls!

My taste in clothes hasn't really changed much since I started modelling in my late teens. None of my friends, family or managers have ever advised me what to wear (probably because they know I wouldn't listen!) but over the years countless stylists have tried to transform me for magazine or newspaper shoots. God it's boring. I'll turn up and they will say, 'Right, we want to make you look completely unlike Jordan – it'll be great!' They seem to think that by putting me in edgy designer clothes and leaving my face free of make-up I'll be magically transformed into someone else. What a load of bollocks. I say to them very clearly, 'I can't bear

An anti-Jordan makeover

these clothes and I hate how you want me to have my make-up and hair, but because this is your shoot and I appreciate you want me to look different I will do it.' In this business I think it's important to be honest about what you think, even if you might offend people. I am always professional and never moan, but I will tell them to hurry up and take the pictures.

I always get asked in interviews if I regret anything I've worn in the past and the honest answer is no, I don't. When I look back at old photos they'll just

remind me of a certain event and why I chose to wear that particular outfit – and what I got up to while I was wearing it! I wouldn't even say I've ever made any fashion mistakes. As far as I'm aware, I've always left the house thinking I looked good. For example, I was slated for wearing a pink rubber catsuit for the Eurovision Song Contest auditions while I was pregnant with Junior, but I loved that outfit at the time and I would definitely still wear it today. I was trying to prove a point – that I could have a bit of a bump but still be sexy – and I think I achieved that. Plus it got people talking, which was exactly what I wanted. Having said that, I do sometimes cringe at certain details of things I've worn in the past, like how high I had the waistband on a pair of trousers, or old glamour

*Check out those
dodgy waistbands*

modelling shots where I've had my knickers pulled right up to my belly button. These days I like my waistbands to be as low as possible – I hate anything that gives me a long-looking bum!

Unlike most celebrities I never follow fashion, as I prefer to look unique. I don't give a toss whether my outfit is 'on trend' or not – I'm proud to have my own personal sense of style. But I do enjoy flicking through glossy magazines like Vogue, Elle and Cosmopolitan to check out what the designers are showing on their catwalks. I usually love the stuff the models are wearing in the shows, as the outfits have been styled to look really outrageous and over the top, but then when I go in the shops I can never find anything I like. It really winds me up.

I love all the different designers, from Chanel to Gucci to Chloé, but I tend to stick to their shoes and bags as their clothes never look quite right on me or don't fit properly. I think Dolce & Gabbana do gorgeous stuff, but they're designed for tiny tits not big-uns like mine! Anyway, it's completely irrelevant to me whether something has a designer label inside. Whether it's New Look or Louis Vuitton, if I see something and I like it – I'll wear it.

*No matter what I'm wearing,
I always like to make the
outfit my own. Wearing just
one sock made this stand out*

INSIDE MY DRESSING ROOM...

At home I've got twelve wardrobes and five chests of drawers filled with clothes, shoes and accessories, plus over 400 pink storage boxes of stuff in my garage and taking up a whole room at my friend's house. I haven't worn most of it; much of it will still have the original labels on. But every day without fail I will go into my dressing room, fling open the wardrobe doors and think, I've got nothing to wear! I just get so bored of looking at the same thing every day. I'll pull something out and hold it up against myself, then chuck it on the floor. Then I'll have another rummage and do it again. This will happen literally dozens of times, with the pile of clothes on the floor getting bigger and bigger, until I finally decide on my outfit which quite often will be the first thing I pulled out anyway!

My wardrobes are actually really well organised, by style and colour. I keep all my casual stuff – the tracksuits, tops and pyjamas which make up the majority of my wardrobe – in my bedroom, and everything else is in my dressing room upstairs. My chests of drawers are neatly divided up with sections for bikinis, baseball caps, scarves, socks, belts and sunglasses. I even have a storage system for my underwear, with my big knickers kept apart from the tiny knickers and so on. I know where everything is – unless my little sister Sophie has been in and nicked something. People laugh at how organised I am – I have a little office at home which is spotlessly neat and ordered – and yet I'll walk in and put my car keys down somewhere then have to play back our security cameras to find out where I left them!

The one thing I don't treat very well is my shoes. God knows how many pairs I've got: thousands and thousands probably, most of them in storage in the garage. Sometimes I'll even buy a pair of shoes not realising I already have them! I hate shoeboxes and never keep them, so all the shoes are piled in a heap on top of each other under the clothes in my wardrobe according to colour, while my handbags are in a storage section at the top. When I buy shoes I like to get the handbags to match, although you'll hardly ever see me wearing them together. I just like the way they look in my wardrobe, and then months and months will go past and I'll realise I've never even used them.

Even though I tend to wear an outfit once then never again, I'm not planning on saving any of my clothes for Princess. I'm starting an eBay site and will sell all my old stuff with a percentage going to charity. But I have kept all the kids' clothes from when they were born and I will never part with them for sentimental reasons. I'm an old softie really.

MY TEN STYLE COMMANDMENTS

1. MAKE SURE YOU MATCH

If I could give you just one piece of style advice it would be this: Match! Not just your clothes, but shoes, jewellery and all your accessories too, right down to your earrings. I always have the same colour nail varnish on my hands and feet and it would really annoy me to wear a bra and knickers from different sets. Even if I'm just slobbing out in pyjamas at home, I'll make sure I match in some way.

All my wardrobes are colour-coordinated, like a rainbow, so I can instantly put an outfit together. If I want to be bright and girlie that morning, I'll head for the pinks, yellows, turquoises or greens. Or I'll find a T-shirt I want to wear, perhaps one with a Care Bear on the front, and I'll pick out the dominant colour on the design then find bottoms and accessories to match.

God knows how many different coloured watches and pairs of sunglasses I've got. I even choose my diamonds to make sure they coordinate with my look. For example, if a ring's got a pink stone in it I wouldn't wear it with a baby blue outfit. Luckily my big diamond ring goes with everything, but it's usually in our safe at home and even I don't know how to unlock it!

Besides, it's not practical to wear it all the time because it's so bloody big.

2. DON'T BE AFRAID OF COLOUR

When it comes to clothes, most people tend to play it safe and stick to one or two boring colours. As you can probably tell, I'm not one of them. I love pretty, girlie shades and will usually wear bright colours as I like to have a happy aura. The more dark colours someone wears, the more depressing I think it looks. Today, for instance, I've got on a bright pink hairband to match my pink nails and the rest of my outfit is green – an Abercrombie tracksuit and little socks. Having said that, whenever I feel at all self-conscious about my body – if I've put on a bit of weight or feel bloated – I always turn to black clothes for their slimming effect. When I was training for the marathon I was pigging out so much I put on loads of weight and generally bulked up from all the running: I went through three pairs of riding boots as my calves got so big. It was while we were living in LA and I was desperate to wear all the sexy, brightly coloured, skintight clothes that I'd packed, but instead I had to cover up in baggy black.

3. GROOMING – IT'S NOT JUST FOR HORSES

It doesn't matter what I'm wearing; as long as my hair and nails are immaculate I feel like I'm ready to face the world. That's what makes me feel properly dressed. You could be wearing the most horrible tracksuit to pop to the shops, but when you go to pay for something at least your hands will look gorgeous. I really hate bitten-down, horrible nails; there's just no excuse for it and it lets down your whole look. If I've chipped a nail – oh my god, I just wouldn't feel happy leaving the house.

So when I'm getting ready I'll always take a bit of time to make sure my hair looks good, even if it's just scraped back in a bobble. I'll check my eyebrows are neatly plucked and grease them with a bit of Vaseline to keep them groomed. I very rarely wear make-up during the day, but if I do it will be foundation, blusher and lip salve for a bit of shine. I do have my eyelashes dyed, but they are naturally curly so mascara isn't essential. See, there is something natural about me! I do have regular massages and facials, but you can get a friend or your other half to do that for you if you can't afford to go to a salon. I find it's always a good quality in a man if he can give a decent foot rub!

– Neat hair and minimal make-up and I'm ready to face the world

Cleanliness is also very important to me. It doesn't matter how much money you've got, you can always make sure you're spotless and sweet-smelling. I'm not a shower person, but I love baths with lots of scented oils and have one at least twice a day. People come round to the house and I'll shout down, 'Come on up, I'm in the bath!' My friends think it's hilarious. It doesn't matter what state I'm in, even when I was on my deathbed after my botched boob reduction I had to get in the bath.

I'm obsessed with washing my clothes too. Even if I've only worn something for a couple of hours it will go straight in the wash, then I'll put two sachets of Bounce in the tumble dryer so everything has that lovely fresh smell. You'll probably think I've got that obsessive–compulsive disorder thing, but I'm not like that – I just like to smell nice.

4. KEEP IT COMFY…

Believe it or not, I don't actually like wearing tight-fitting stuff unless I'm going somewhere I know I'm going to be photographed. I'll wear a Wonderbra when I go out, but as soon as I get home I'll have to take it off and put a sports one on. It might not be sexy, but I'd much rather be comfortable when I'm lounging around the house. In fact, I'll often spend the whole day in pyjamas (clean ones, obviously…) as it just makes me feel more relaxed. I have a whole wardrobe of PJs – I even take them with me whenever I'm flying anywhere to change into on the plane. Whenever friends come round to my house I like them to be comfy too, so I'll ask them to bring their pyjamas or trackies and get changed when they arrive.

5. … BUT SUFFER TO BE STUNNING

Comfort is important, unless I'm going somewhere where I want to make an impression, in which case I will happily put up with all sorts of pain

to look drop-dead fabulous. If I know I'm going to be photographed I'll be breathing in like crazy so I know my body looks its best. At my wedding I wore three huge hairpieces and a jewelled crown to walk down the aisle. It was bloody heavy I can tell you, but it was worth it for the effect. And when it comes to heels, I do think higher equals sexier. Just make sure you've got a taxi on standby – or a willing bloke to massage your feet at the end of the night!

Glamourpuss from the knees up, cosy from the knees down

6. DON'T BE A SLAVE TO FASHION

I would never, ever wear something just because it's considered to be in fashion. I've always gone for clothes that make me stand out, rather than blend in with the rest of the crowd. I would hate to look the same as everyone else. I would rather be in a magazine with a big cross next to my outfit than be in one of those 'Who wore it best?' features where they compare two celebrities who've been pictured out at an event wearing something identical. I can guarantee you'll never see me in something like that. I'll always customise an outfit with diamante studs or cut it up to create something completely unique. Having said that, I do sometimes mix something really fashionable with my usual style clothes. I might stick on a pair of trendy skinny jeans, but I'll wear them with a cute pink hoodie and matching flip-flops so that the look is all my own.

7. NEVER WORRY ABOUT THE WEATHER – OR WHAT OTHER PEOPLE THINK

I've never let anyone tell me what to wear. Nowadays I will occasionally ask friends what they think of an outfit if I'm going out, but they'll know there is no point in saying 'You can't go out looking like that', because they know that if I want to wear it, I will.

I know I'm always on the worst-dressed lists or pictured in magazines and labelled vile for what I wear, but you know what? I don't give a toss. Anyway, I can't win. I might be wearing some gorgeous designer dress that's worth thousands, but just because it's on Katie Price it's not credible to say that it looks good.

It's not just other people's opinions; the time of year has no effect on what I wear either. Regardless of what the weather is, in my head it's always warm and sunny – the central heating is always on full blast at home anyway. So if it's really dull outside but I want to wear something bright and summery, then I'll do it. I do hate being cold though – and I don't do coats – so if I have to go out I'll be in the car with the heating full on, snuggled up with my blanket and pillow, and will drive right up to wherever I'm going and just run in. Then it doesn't really matter if I'm wearing hot pants and flip-flops when there's snow on the ground.

8. CONFIDENCE IS KEY

When it comes to style, I don't agree with rules that say you can't wear a short skirt if you're bigger than a size 10 or whatever. No matter what size or shape you are, carrying off an outfit is all about inner confidence. If you're a big girl and you want to wear a tiny little dress then as long as you're immaculately groomed and feel good about yourself people will just think how fabulous you look. But if you don't feel sure of yourself it will show in your aura. Even now I

know I've got love handles and so there are things I wouldn't feel happy wearing. I look at shapely girls like J.Lo and Beyoncé and think, If I were that big I wouldn't have the balls to wear something so revealing. But they are obviously so confident and comfortable with themselves they just look fantastic and sexy.

9. DON'T FORGET TO LOOK IN THE MIRROR – FROM ALL ANGLES!

I'm sorry, but when I see some people I just think, Did you actually look in the mirror before leaving the house? There's being confident, and then there's being deluded. A 50-year-old woman can wear a tight dress and not look like mutton, but only if it is done with a bit of class. No disrespect to Pamela Anderson, but she's been wearing a lot of really short stuff recently and I just don't think she's actually looked in the mirror to see what her behind looks like. You really shouldn't have it all on show when you've got such bad cellulite. I see some women wearing tiny little tops and low-cut jeans, but they've got stretch marks all over their bellies. I know there's nothing you can do about scars, but do you really need to show them off? These women probably think people are staring at them because they're looking hot, whereas what they're actually thinking is, Bloody hell, how horrific are those stretch marks? You've got to be realistic.

10. YOU DON'T HAVE TO SPLASH THE CASH TO LOOK GOOD

Whenever I go into shops the assistants immediately direct me to the most expensive stuff. It drives me mad. Just because I've got money it doesn't mean I'm going to spend twelve grand on a dress. I've come from nothing and worked hard to get what I've got, so why splash it about on something I'll wear once then stuff in a box in my garage? Anyway, these days the high street is so good you can look fabulous on a tight budget. I will have the odd splurge though. The other day I spent seventeen grand on Versace bedding at Harrods. It was ridiculous. I just thought, Well, I better have the best f-ing sleep ever!

MY TOP 10 WARDROBE ESSENTIALS

Tracksuit
What I wear most of the time

T-shirt
I like them either studded with crystals, or decorated with a cartoon, or both

A stretchy hairband
Essential for less-than-perfect hair days

Leggings
I like to wear them with a long, fitted T-shirt for a sleek silhouette

Loose jersey dress
In a bright colour, can easily be dressed up or down

Ugg boots
Most men seem to hate them but I live in mine

Flip-flops
I've got them in every colour and studded with Swarovski crystals

Platform heels
As high as you can cope with!

Costume jewellery
An easy way to add colour to an outfit

Legwarmers
For that fun, Flashdance vibe

STYLE CRIMES!

Ankle-swingers
Too-short trousers are just tragic

White socks with black shoes
Unless you're in a slutty schoolgirl outfit

Bitten nails and bad hygiene
There's no excuse for it

High-waisted things
Low-rise jeans and skirts are more flattering

Head-to-toe black
Bright colours are so much more fun – unless you're having a fat day

MY DESERT ISLAND ESSENTIALS

Hairband, lip salve, toothbrush, bikini, dressing gown and flip-flops

2

Jordan

OK, let's start by getting one thing straight. Despite what the press make out, I don't have these two opposite personalities – classy, feminine Katie Price and super-slut Jordan – fighting for attention inside me. They are exactly the same person. I suppose if there is a difference between Kate and Jordan, it's all in the attitude. Or to put it another way: if Jordan is posing for a photo she will sit there with her legs at quarter to three, whereas Katie Price will have them at half past six!

People have asked if I created the character of Jordan as a way of getting back at all the men who'd treated me badly in my life: the abusive boyfriend, the paedophile photographer, the pervert who assaulted me in a park when I was a little girl. Perhaps there is something in that – who knows? When I was younger, dressing up in sexy little outfits with my boobs on show certainly made me feel powerful: guys could look but they couldn't touch.

But when I first adopted the name Jordan it wasn't because I had planned to create an outrageous alter ego. It was shortly before my first appearance on Page 3 at the age of 18, and my then agent Samantha Bond suggested I come up with a different name to Katie, as at that time doing Page 3 could stop you getting other modelling work. Sam's assistant suggested Jordan, I liked how it sounded and the name stuck. So over the next few years I became infamous for being Jordan: the bolshie, sexy, bad girl who loved clubbing and outrageous outfits. Never mind that I spent most of the time in tracksuits and no make-up when I was out of the public eye; people

assumed this wild character that the press created – and loved to hate – was really me. It wasn't until I went on the ITV1 reality show I'm A Celebrity… Get Me Out of Here! in 2004, when I went by my real name for the first time on TV, that people saw a different side of me and started to refer to me as Katie Price. So I suppose it's not really surprising that nowadays when I put on a skimpy outfit that shows a bit of cleavage for a night out suddenly everyone thinks, Uh oh, Jordan's back. For me, though, I wear that sort of thing as it gets me in the mood for a good party – and the longer it's been since my last big

night out, the sluttier and more over the top my outfit will be. I get dressed up as I love the sexy little skirts, big hair and high heels that I can't wear during the day when I'm running round after the kids (and because I wouldn't feel right going out for a dance in a pair of trousers), not because I've decided I want to 'become' Jordan for the night. But for the purposes of this book, let's call the skimpier, outrageous end of my wardrobe the Jordan look.

One of my all-time favourite Jordan outfits was the costume I wore to my Pimps and Prostitutes-themed 25th birthday party in 2003. The frilly bra, knickers and ripped fishnets with high heels ticked all the right boxes – sexy, adventurous and definitely attention-grabbing! I would still wear something like that on a night out (in fact my dress sense still hasn't really changed since I was 18) but these days I'm more likely to show off my legs than my cleavage. When I first had my boobs done I had them on display pretty

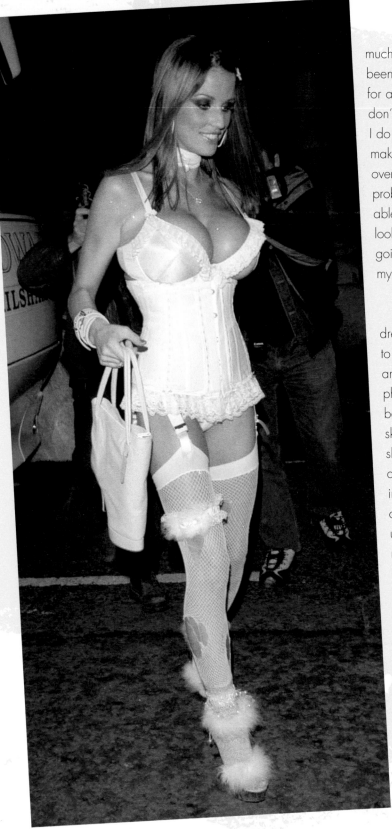

much all of the time, but now it's a case of been there, done that. When you've had them for as many years as I have you realise you don't have to flaunt them to be sexy – although I do admit I still do that sometimes! I just love making the most of what I've got and being over the top with what I wear, because I've probably only got a few years left of being able to carry off the skimpy outfits before looking like mutton: believe me, I won't be going clubbing in a bikini and legwarmers in my 50s.

It goes without saying that if you want to dress like Jordan, you'll need Jordan's balls to carry it off. I will happily stand in a bra and G-string in front of dozens of photographers as I have always loved being the centre of attention, but wearing skimpy clothes isn't necessarily about being skinny or having the perfect figure; it's about having the self-confidence to strut into a nightclub believing you look drop-dead gorgeous. One of my girlfriends used to be a lot bigger than me but on nights out she'd still wear these little skirts and tiny tops – proper tits-out style. But because she had this don't-give-a-shit attitude she looked fantastic and oozed sex appeal. It doesn't matter what size you are, if you feel confident in what you're wearing that will shine through. If you genuinely believe you can get away with it (although as I said before, it's important to be realistic about your body and take an honest look in the mirror)

My Pimps and Prostitutes themed 25th birthday party

Hello Boys!

then wear it, and don't worry about what other people might think. I can walk into a really classy place when I'm wearing something outrageous and you can see people thinking, I bet she's a hooker. But it doesn't bother me, as I know I don't have to prove anything to anyone. People will always have different opinions, and that's just fine with me. You definitely have to learn to be strong like that and I know it can be hard, but it helps if you have a couple of drinks with the girls while you're getting ready to go out. I might pick out a nice sensible outfit, but once I've had a vodka or two I'll think, Nah, I'm going slutty tonight!

I do find it hugely flattering when girls want to dress like me. I don't mind being copied at all – in fact I absolutely love it. I'm not sure if my personal style has had anything to do with it, but over the past ten years I have noticed that young girls seem to be dressing much sexier. People like the Pussycat Dolls now do the little hot pants, legwarmers and ankle socks thing that I've been doing for years. The only thing that annoys me is when girls steal my style to try and become famous. Take that Chantelle Houghton. When she first went on Celebrity Big Brother a few years ago she had her own individual look, but a few months later her hair, make-up and style of dress started to look more and more like mine. I just don't see why she needed to copy someone else; she already had had her own identity, so nicking mine just made her look stupid.

BECOMING JORDAN

I'll start getting ready for a night out by having a soak in a nice deep bath with lots of bubbles and scented oils. I don't have to wash my hair myself very often, as I do so many shoots it's usually been professionally blow-dried by a stylist, so I keep it dry inside a shower cap while I'm in the bath. When I get out I'll slather on lots of body lotion to match whatever perfume I'll be wearing, then I'll rub in some body shimmer on top of that for extra glitz and definition. It's a really good trick for making your legs and arms look more shapely.

I don't ever spend hours getting dressed and doing my hair and make-up; in fact if I'm really pressed for time I could be out of the door in half an hour, although that would be a real rush. But if the girls have come round and we're all getting ready together then it takes me bloody ages. I'll stick my iPod on shuffle, so we get 1980s cheese, more modern dance tracks and ballads all mixed up to get us in the mood for a party and we'll be laughing and trying on different stuff while having a few drinks. Usually I'll be going out with my sister Sophie and a handful of my oldest friends, none of whom are famous or work in the industry, but whoever it is they'll always know they're in for a big night. If you come out with the Pricey, you'd better cancel work the next day or be prepared to go in late as you're gonna get wrecked!

My make-up artist and best friend Gary usually does my make-up, as more often than not he'll be coming out with us too, but if I'm doing my own I have a very quick routine. I'll put on foundation and groom my eyebrows, then apply blusher, lip gloss and mascara. And I'm a big fan of false lashes – the bigger, the better. As I rarely wear much make-up during the day, I like to pile it on when I'm wearing my trashy little outfits on a night out. The Jordan look is all about big hair and big eyes, so sometimes I'll wear three pairs of lashes at once piled on top of each other. I find wearing falsies much speedier than putting on loads of mascara, which can end up getting smudged and takes ages to remove at the end of the night.

I don't ever take make-up with me when I go to a club, apart from a tube of lip gloss, because if I want

a bit of blusher or whatever while I'm out my friends will usually be carrying some. Or if I'm in the toilets at a club, like any girl, I'll just ask if I can borrow someone else's.

Although my hair is regularly blow-dried I'll usually decide it isn't big enough and so I'll add volume with hairpieces. I don't think there has ever been a Jordan-inspired drag queen (actually there was one once, but she was pretty crap – I think her name was Jodie Marsh) but I certainly look like one sometimes!

Although I love revealing outfits, I've never used tit tape. When you've had a boob job it's important to look after them properly, so I don't like to let them just hang there without any support. Instead, I keep them perked up and looking their best with my trusty Wonderbra. And I've never been one of these desperate girls who'll deliberately go out without any knickers and then flash the paparazzi to try and get in the papers. If I'm wearing a short skirt I'll always keep my bits covered up, even if it's just a tiny little G-string. There's nothing worse than seeing a knicker-line through your clothes though, so if I'm wearing a really tight dress I will occasionally go commando – and I have been caught out a couple of times unintentionally. I once wore a polo-neck leopard-skin Roberto Cavalli dress to the Gina Shoes 50th birthday party. It was dead tight and down to my knees, so I didn't wear anything underneath, but somehow the paparazzi got a shot. Well, they do all lie on the street trying to point their cameras up your skirt…

My choice of outfit will depend on all sorts of things, like whether I'm bloated because I'm due on or if I've eaten too much. I hate having my belly on show at the best of times, unless I'm feeling particularly good about my body, as I'm conscious of having to breathe it in all night to keep it looking flat. But even if I'm feeling a bit blobby, it won't stop me going for something revealing. I might wear a backless top that's baggier at the front with a tiny miniskirt: that way I can hide my belly, but still show off some skin and look sexy.

The 'Jordan' outfits I wear for nights out are often quite expensive. For instance, I wore a black and white PVC schoolgirl dress and stockings earlier this year for a night out at the London club Movida and that was £300. But I promise you don't need to spend a lot of money on your clothes to look cheap! I usually buy my glam going-out gear in sex shops or catalogues like Leg Avenue, which specialises in adult-oriented costumes – sexy Little Red Riding Hoods and kinky pirates, that sort of thing – and whenever I'm in Los Angeles I stock up with loads of fun, frilly stuff at a fabulous place called Trashy Lingerie. If you don't feel confident enough to visit sex shops, try fancy dress stores for naughty nurse or French maid outfits, or just

buy stretchy tops or mini dresses in really small sizes so they come up extra tight. If I'm stuck for inspiration, I'll often have a dig round my wardrobe and find something that I can cut short and customise to make a completely different outfit. I actually buy quite a lot of my clothes in kids' shops too because the length is often better on me. I'm quite short, so if I buy an adult size 8 skirt I'll usually have to take it

Covering up my belly but still flashing flesh

up. My skirts always have to be exactly nine inches long. For me it's the perfect length – not too long, and just short enough to get away with!

There's one final thing I'll always take with me when I go on a night out clubbing: a security guard. People might not know this, but there's a big difference between red-carpet paparazzi and the paparazzi you get hanging around outside nightclubs. The latter are just stalkers with a camera and will try every dirty trick in the book to get a photo, so I like to have security with me to help me get in and out of the club safely

My sexy schoolgirl look complete with my must-have clubbing accessory – a security guard

One of my sexy Leg Avenue numbers

and deal with any fights. Also, as much as I love my fans, if my friends are out with me it can be very annoying for them if people keep coming up the whole time asking for autographs and photos when we're trying to have a dance or a quiet chat, which is usually what happens when I go to a club. So these days I'll always take a bloke with me. Not some huge, seven-foot man-mountain like the bouncers you see with Britney and Beyoncé; personally I think good people skills is a more important quality in a security guard.

ESSENTIAL ADVICE FOR A BIG NIGHT OUT, JORDAN-STYLE

1. HOW TO KEEP FALSE EYELASHES ON ALL NIGHT

The trick to getting false lashes to stay put is to apply a little eyelash glue (I just use the normal stuff) along the strip and then blow on it a bit, until it's nearly dry and feels a bit tacky. Don't put the lashes straight on after applying the glue or they'll slip all over the place and drop in your vodka Red Bull.

2. HOW TO WALK IN SIX-INCH HEELS

There is no limit to the height of heels I will wear for a night out. I love towering platforms and sky-high stilettos. I admit I'm lucky, as I get a car from home to the club so I don't usually have to move about much in my heels – apart from a bit of dancing at my table! But if you know you'll be on your feet a lot you could try experimenting with those little gel pads you slip in your shoes, or carry a pair of flip-flops in your bag.

3. LOOKING GOOD IN THE BRITISH WEATHER

Remember, girls, if you're going out and you want to look good it's not about feeling comfortable, it's about making a statement. And a great big Puffa jacket doesn't exactly scream glamour, does it? I hate being cold, but I never need to wear a coat as I don't have to walk around the streets. I always make sure I have my duvet and a pillow in the car and a pair of pyjamas to change into on my way home.

My signature pose is looking over my shoulder…

…or doing a cheeky wink…

…or pouting…

…and sometimes I do them all at once!

4. HOW TO LOOK YOUR BEST IN PHOTOS

Although I've been modelling for years, I'm not very good at looking natural in informal snapshots. It's not that I'm camera-shy, it's just that when my friends get out their cameras I automatically go into model mode and start posing. My signature pose is looking back over one shoulder, but you could try doing a cheeky wink or pouting your lips as if you are gently blowing bubbles. Whatever pose I do though, I always remember to breathe in to look thinner. It's hard to do this without your ribcage sticking out, but a little trick I use it to imagine there's a string attached to my belly button, which then I pull back towards my spine. You just have to make sure you don't hunch your shoulders up while you're doing it.

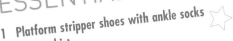

MY 5 JORDAN ESSENTIALS

1 Platform stripper shoes with ankle socks
2 A tiny skirt
3 Tiny top with a Wonderbra
4 Hairpieces
5 Catsuit

A hairpiece and stripper shoes are key but the swan is optional

WHAT'S IN MY HANDBAG?

Credit card, mobile phone, lip gloss – and that's it!

5. HOW TO DEAL WITH SLEAZY BLOKES

If you wear the sort of outfits I do then you're really going to have to be prepared for the fact that you might attract the wrong kind of men. But who are you dressing for anyway? The Jordan look is all about expressing yourself with make-up and clothes, not trying to look a certain way to please a bloke. But remember: even though you might be dressed like a cheap tart, it doesn't mean you have to act like one. If you hit it off with a guy in a club, never sleep with them that night – no matter how drunk you are. One night stands are a big mistake. It is important to let them see you in the daytime in a sober state and your normal dress before letting them get you into bed.

Out with my good pal Michelle Heaton

MY PERFECT NIGHT OUT

My favourite club
Movida in London's West End

My friends
As well as my sister and old Brighton friends, I love going clubbing with Gary and Phil. They're my two best friends and Princess's godparents – I call them her fairy godmothers! I have a right laugh with Michelle Heaton too, but she lives in Ireland so it's a bit hard to see her regularly

The song that always gets me dancing
'Wifey' by Next

My favourite drink
I do like a strawberry daiquiri. I can't drink them all night, but they get me in a party mood and then I'll move onto vodka and Coke

And finally...
Like most people, if I'm not in too much of a state we'll get a doner kebab or a burger on the way home. Love it! But I won't remember eating it until I see my clothes the next day...

3

Yummy Mummy

I'll let you into a little secret: whenever I'm pregnant, I go blonde. I've got no idea why, but about the same time that little blue line appears on the pregnancy test I'll usually be reaching for the bleach. Weird, eh? I was thinking about lightening my hair up a bit the other day, and it's probably no coincidence that I'm feeling very broody at the moment…

Oh, I just love being a mum. I think it's the best job in the world, I want to have at least seven or eight kids. A whole brood running round the house! The only problem is I bloody hate being pregnant. The gross bump, the mood swings, the puking: for me it's nine months of pure hell, although of course it is worth it for the incredible end result. Having said

that, I actually sort of enjoyed being pregnant with Harvey. I think it's because I was single at the time, having split from Harvey's dad Dwight Yorke, so I could do exactly what I wanted, when I wanted. I was still going riding and had a really good social life, plus I wasn't anywhere near as sick as I was during my second and third pregnancies. With Harvey I was never physically sick, it was more like a sort of constant nausea which was bad enough, but with Junior I was chucking up all day, every day, for months on end. I remember being in the car on the way to jobs and my driver Rob would have to keep pulling over for me to lean out of the window and be sick. It was just as bad with Princess. Not only that, but each time I've been pregnant I've got bigger and bigger – I put on a

At the Brit Awards, pregnant with Junior but trying to hide my bump

stone and a half with Harvey, two stone with Junior and a whopping three stone with Princess – and as the size of my bump has increased so has my sciatica. God, I was in agony with Princess; I had shooting pains down both sides of my body. Pete was very sweet and understanding when I struggled with morning sickness, back pain and mood swings during my pregnancies with Junior and Princess. I reckon men sometimes think that women play on being pregnant to get sympathy, but when he saw me being physically sick he knew I wasn't joking – I really did feel rotten.

One mistake I've made with past pregnancies that I definitely won't be making again is that I've tried to

keep the baby a secret until I'm quite far gone. The early days are stressful enough without having to struggle to hide your bump and make constant excuses if you're sick or moody, when really all you want to do is scream, 'I'm pregnant, I feel like shit, I'm knackered – just bloody leave me alone!' I know you're advised to wait until twelve weeks to tell people because of the risk of miscarriage, but those first three months are when you feel at your worst and are most in need of sympathy.

I guess some people must think mums-to-be are more womanly or sexy, but I just feel fat and frumpy. I do like having a neat little bump in the early stages and I'm quite lucky in that I only seem to gain weight on my belly, so from behind you can't even tell I'm pregnant. But believe me, there's nothing remotely sexy about me when I'm stuck in bed with a huge bump, moaning like an old lady because I can't move. My boobs don't even get bigger, they just get really veiny. Yuck. And although I don't get stretch marks, my post-baby belly looks a right old state. The skin looks like jelly and I've got this sort of hole where my stomach muscles never went back together, so whenever I eat anything my tummy sticks out and I look pregnant again.

MY CRAVINGS...

Harvey – Monster Munch and soup
Junior – ice cubes and jacket potatoes
Princess – ice cubes and roast dinners

DRESSING MY BUMP

When I'm pregnant I try to keep my style pretty much the same as usual, although because I feel so ugly I usually pile on the make-up and have more sunbeds – anything to make me feel a little bit more attractive. When I was pregnant with Junior I kept on having regular Botox injections as no one suggested it might harm the baby, but with Princess I decided not to, simply because the doctors said they still weren't sure of the side effects – and once I was aware of that, I

didn't want to take the risk. Most people seem to get it in their heads that just because they're pregnant they have to buy maternity wear, but I think those tent-like smocks make you look even bigger. I tend to buy normal tops but in a bigger size, say a 12 or 14, as I prefer to wear things that are fitted. It helps that I've had all my babies in the summer, so I can wear little vests and cropped cardigans that show off the bump. I never gain weight on my legs, so I wear my usual bottoms and push them down under my

belly, and if I can't do up my jeans I'll just tie a hair elastic around the button to keep them up. I'll even wear heels while heavily pregnant, but only for about an hour at a time – any longer than that and it gets seriously uncomfortable.

During my first pregnancy I was far more outrageously dressed than with the others, purely because I was single and still looking for a proper relationship. I wanted to give off the impression that I might be pregnant but I'm still sexy and you can still go for me. Looking back, it was an insecurity thing: I was worried no one would fancy me because I was expecting

What was I thinking when I wore this gold number to the Ali G film premiere?

although, as everyone knows, a certain spiky-haired Pop Idol proved me wrong on that front! I remember a photo of me at the Ali G movie premiere when I was pregnant with Harvey: I was wearing a shiny gold two-piece outfit with my boobs and bump hanging out, heavy make-up and cheap, brassy blonde hair extensions with the thick glue bonds showing and dark roots. Gross. At the

I'm still wearing my normal jeans but have covered the gap with some sparkly material to match my hairband

HELLO MUMMY!

There's no denying that those early days of motherhood are absolutely knackering, but I can honestly say that even in the depths of post-natal depression I have always made sure I've got washed and dressed every day. I know some women let themselves go a bit in the early days of motherhood, but I could never stop making an effort with my appearance. The way I look at it, you might feel like shit but being dirty and scruffy is hardly going to make you feel better about yourself, is it? I like to be a yummy mummy, not a minging mum!

If you've had a Caesarean you'll need to keep the scar dry for a while, but I'll just have a shallow bath or have a strip wash instead. I don't breastfeed, but that's only because I'm usually going straight back to work and also I think it's nice for dads to be able to take part in the feeding to help them bond with the bubba. As for my beauty routine, when you've just had a baby I think it's more important than ever to make sure you take care of the basics. It might be the last thing you feel like doing, but making the effort to treat yourself to a professional manicure will not only make you look better, it will boost your mood. Make sure your eyebrows are neatly plucked and tinted, too. It doesn't cost much and on those days when you can't be bothered to put on any make-up (which is most of them, if you're anything like me) a well-shaped set of brows frames your face and instantly gives you a fresh look. Add a bit of lip gloss and you're good to go. As for your hair, ponytails are a new mum's best friend, so make sure you're stocked up with hair bobbles and bands.

I just don't understand why some celebrities get all dolled up in a sexy little dress and high heels for a day out with their kids. If they're anything like me, they'll be chasing round after the children, bending

Everyone told me not to wear this but I wanted to make sure I got a reaction

time I loved it, although now I just think I looked trashy.

My maternity style has become less slutty in later pregnancies, as I was happy and no longer needed to give off the 'I'm available' vibes. Don't get me wrong, I still like to dress up and flash a bit of flesh — on some occasions a bit too much. When I was pregnant with Junior, I was invited to the British Comedy Awards. I was feeling particularly fat and ugly at the time and thought that wearing something revealing would make me feel sexier, so I chose a black dress with the sides completely cut away and held together with buckles. I remember when I was getting ready to go out everyone was saying, 'Oh no, Kate, don't', but I was adamant that being pregnant wouldn't stop me dressing how I wanted. Why the hell should I cover myself up just because I'm expecting? I'm not ill, I'm pregnant. I think most women feel like that, although they probably wouldn't be as daring as me! Anyway, I walked out onto the stage to present this award I remember hearing the whole audience gasp in shock. And I admit that I look at that picture now, with everything on show and that bright blonde hair, and think, Oh my god, what a state!

MY PREGNANCY WARDROBE ESSENTIALS

Comfy shoes
Uggs and flip-flops
Socks
Give me a pair of snugly cashmere socks
and I'm a happy girl
Tracksuit bottoms
Obviously!
Maternity jeans
The one maternity wear item I think it's worth investing
in. I bought a pair with a stretchy panel that you pull over
the bump: sooo comfy...
A long T-shirt
If you've got stretch marks and don't want to show
off your belly, you can wear this layered with vests
and leggings for a covered-up but sleek look
A proper bra
I wear sports bras while pregnant, and sleep
in them too

Princess's proud mummy

MY PREGNANCY PAMPERING REGIME

★ Throughout my pregnancies I rubbed Decleor body oil on my belly every evening to prevent stretch marks. I loved the smell (although I can't stand it when I'm not pregnant) and it always used to make the baby move, which I loved. But I do think that if you're prone to getting stretch marks you'll get them no matter what you do. I don't have them, neither does my mum, but some of my friends had far smaller bumps than me, used creams and oils religiously and they still got them. Still, at least your skin will be soft...

★ To help my sciatica, I had weekly massages. Obviously it's difficult to lie on your front when you're pregnant, but I put a rolled-up towel under my boobs and hips to support my belly during the treatment. It's so comforting having a massage while pregnant that someone should invent a couch with a bump-shaped hole in it!

★ I have reflexology throughout my pregnancies. I don't really believe in the theory behind it, I just love having my feet massaged. People say it helps the baby come out, but I've tried everything – deep reflexology, curries, sex – and none of it works. When the baby's ready, it's ready.

★ I know not everyone likes to look orange like me, but when you're pregnant you can look so pale and drained a tan can really give you a boost. Plus, it covers up all the veins which pop up when you're preggy. If you don't want to go on a sunbed, try fake tan for a healthy glow. I guarantee it will make you look better.

★ Whether I'm pregnant or not, I'll shave my legs, arms, armpits and my bits every day. Yes, even with a big bump in the way I make sure I'm perfectly smooth down there! I've been doing it so long that I can just guess what I'm doing and – touch wood – I've never had worse than a couple of minor nicks. But if you're not confident you could get your partner to do it, although personally I don't really fancy the idea of anyone going at my bits with a razor!

★ Finally, I always make sure I get my hair blow-dried shortly before the birth. Believe me, you'll need all the help you can get in those first post-birth baby photos...

down to pick up stuff they've dropped and carrying them when they get tired: impossible if you're tottering around on platforms. For instance, if we're going out for a day at a theme park the last thing I want to do is worry about getting in and out of the rides elegantly or getting my dry-clean-only designer dress soaked on the water slide. So when I'm out with the children it's tracksuits all the way. I do sometimes plan to make an effort and go out in a nice pair of jeans and shoes, but then in the morning I'll look in my wardrobe and think, Nah, I just want to be comfy, and so on goes the trackie again. I'm such a chav!

DRESSING THE KIDS

I spend far more money on the children's clothes than I do on my own, as I'd much rather spoil them. We get most of their stuff in Harrods, as they have lots of designer concessions where you can get really unusual stuff, or on shopping trips when we visit America.

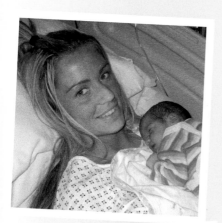

I might just have given birth to Junior but at least my hair looks ok

HARVEY

I buy a lot of D&G and Topman for Harvey. I think it's so unfair when you see disabled kids dressed in vile clothes, so I try to dress him as trendily as I can. Everyone laughs, because I'll make sure he's always got his Calvin Klein boxers over his nappies! It's far easier to dress Harvey now he's lost weight, but he's still big for his age so I'll buy adult-sized True Religion jeans and cut the legs shorter so they fit. Thank god I'm handy with a sewing machine. Harvey went through a stage where he couldn't stand things with buttons and he likes to undo zips, so I tend to avoid clothes with complicated fastenings and go for elasticated waists instead.

MY DAY-OUT BAG FOR THE KIDS

A change of clothes for each child
Nappies for Harvey and Princess
Pyjamas for all three of them
Bottles
Snacks – raisins, fruit, biscuits
Wipes
A toy each
A couple of books
Harvey's medicine bag

JUNIOR

I dress Junior in the sort of trendy clothes I like to see adult guys wearing – a hoodie with jeans, a T-shirt and a nice little beanie, for example. I always try to make him wear his jeans on his hips with the top of his boxer shorts peeping out the top, but he's going through a stage where he pulls the waistband right up so they look like ankle-swingers. It's so annoying – I'm forever yanking them down again. And it takes me ages to get him dressed, because if he had his way he would spend all day in pyjamas. He must get that from his mum! I've been getting Junior's hair highlighted for a while now; in fact it looks odd if he doesn't have a bit of colour in there. He loves having his highlights done, but he can't stand having gel in his hair and goes absolutely nuts if I try to put any in it. His hair is cut in a style that needs a bit of product, so I have to cover my hands with gel then call him over and pretend to give his hair an affectionate ruffle so he doesn't realise that I've done it.

A born show-off, just like his mum

PRINCESS

Thankfully, Princess is a true girlie girl. She loves having her nails painted and waves her hands saying 'Pretty, pretty!' if she wants them done. She's already got three wardrobes full of gorgeous clothes, but whenever I dress her up in little skirts and tights I worry she won't be comfy, so I usually end up putting her in tracksuits and glittery tops like a little Katie clone. We've got matching lilac True Religion tracksuits that we wear with our matching pink Uggs; I've even got her these little fake Louis Vuitton bags which she can just fit her dummy and sparkly bracelets in. And yes, I know she'll probably rebel against all the pink and glitter and become a tomboy in a few years' time, but at least I'll know I've had my fun dressing her until then! Whatever happens though, she's definitely not cutting her hair. She's inherited those curls from me, although I was pretty much bald until I was two. Her hair can sometimes look a bit of a fuzz ball, but I've found the perfect frizz-taming treatment:

On the shoot for this book, Princess loved having her nails painted and putting rollers in her hair

I can't wait until I can share Princess's wardrobe

I use a nail treatment called Solar Oil, which is a blend of jojoba and almond oil, and if I put a little bit in Princess' hair it makes the curl nice and defined. Now if only she'd stop pulling out her sparkly hairclips whenever I put them in it would be perfect!

While I obviously love dressing Princess in pretty clothes and painting her nails, I will be doing my best to make sure she doesn't grow up too fast. I think it's vile when you see tiny babies with pierced ears, so I definitely won't be doing that until she's old enough to make the decision to get them done herself. And I hate seeing 12-year-olds looking like mini grown-ups in make-up, short skirts and high heels; that's just plain wrong. I know it's hard in today's society, but I want Princess to enjoy her childhood and being a little girl for as long as possible.

4

Celebrity

'KATIE, KATIE, OVER HERE! OI, JORDAN – THIS WAY, LOOK OVER HERE! GO ON, KATIE, SMILE LOVE! JORDAN!'

Pushing my shoulders back and my boobs out,
    while breathing in to keep my belly as flat as possible, I smile and pose for the bank of photographers lining the red carpet. Around me, other celebrities are chatting to journalists and TV crews waiting in a roped-off area, or being hurried straight into the party by their publicists. Everyone is dressed up in designer gowns and borrowed diamonds. Glamorous? Yes, of course. But at the end of the day, premieres and parties are still work. And believe me, when I'm posing on the red carpet I'm certainly not thinking, Wow, check me out. I'm more likely to be wondering what I'll be getting the kids for tea, or whether I'll be home in time for X Factor.

    To be honest, I'm not really a red carpet kind of girl. When you're in the public eye you get invited to all sorts of glamorous showbiz events, but if I'm going out I prefer to be somewhere I can have a relaxed drink and a giggle with some mates, rather than having to talk to journalists or sit through a long awards

ceremony. But like any girl, I do love any excuse to get glammed up.

Different types of red carpets require different outfits, obviously. For instance, I would never wear a ball gown to a film premiere. You might not realise that when you go to a big movie premiere it's really just like any old trip to the cinema – except there will probably be more famous people in the audience than there are at your local Odeon – so you'd feel a

I absolutely loved this fairytale frock I wore to the Royal Variety Performance

bit of a twat if you were sitting there with your popcorn all dolled up in a big dress. Some people do, but I guess they must need the column inches more than I do... On the other hand, charity balls are the perfect excuse to go for full-on fairytale glamour, so why go in something you might wear to nip down the shops to pick up a pint of milk? But whatever I wear when I'm attending a celebrity event, it will always be chosen with an eye to what the effect will be when I'm walking down that line of paparazzi, and what the resulting pictures will look like. That's not to say I'll spend all day getting ready, it's just that what you wear can speak volumes – and I want to make sure I'm giving off the right messages when I hit the red carpet.

After days of roughing it in the jungle, I was desperate for a bit of girlie glamour

IF CLOTHES COULD TALK...

Dukes of Hazzard premiere

I generally don't make a huge effort for film premieres. I'll wear an outfit that's a bit showy, but nothing too outrageous – unless I've got a point to make of course. When I went to the premiere of The Dukes of Hazzard movie in 2005 it was about six weeks after I gave birth to Junior, and I wanted to prove to everyone that I'd got my figure back. So I wore a pair of tiny hot pants, a little crop top and cowboy boots. The outfit was revealing enough to show I'd lost all my baby weight, plus it went with the film's Western theme. I hate showing off my belly at the best of times so I was breathing in like mad all night, but at least I made my point.

British Book Awards

I had two red carpet events in one day: the prestigious British Book Awards, where I was presenting one of the prizes, and a party for lads' mag Loaded at a London nightclub where I was getting an award for being their Cover Girl of the Decade. Now I could hardly wear the same thing for both, as the audiences at either event couldn't be

From literary vamp...

...to lads mag vixen

more different, but I thought it would make a great set of photos if I wore two versions of the same outfit to both. So Isabell Kristensen, the designer who made my wedding dress, created a long sequinned gown for the formal book event and a short playsuit in the same style and material for the Loaded bash. I wanted to prove I could dress classily just as easily as I could do slutty, and sure enough the pictures were all over the papers next day. Job done.

Andy Wong's Chinese New Year Party

God, I spent ages trying to decide what to wear on this night. Pete and I had been invited to businessman Andy Wong's annual Chinese New Year party, a really glamorous affair with socialites and royalty among the guests. But there was a fancy dress theme, so I knew I could go for something a bit more outrageous than I usually would to that sort of a do. Plus Pete and I were going through a difficult time in our relationship – I was battling post-natal depression and we were arguing a lot – and I admit I was out to let my hair down and have a bloody good time. In the end, I must have been the most cheaply dressed person in the room: the skintight black and silver dress I wore was just twenty quid from a sex shop. Even my G-string (which you could see clearly through the dress) was more expensive!

World Music Awards

I absolutely adore the full-on fairytale look. Give me a dress with lots of diamante, ruffles and a long train and I'm a very happy girl. This was at the World Music Awards in 2006 and I felt so good about how I looked. I loved my hair, my make-up and of course the dress, which is from Doly by Dany Mizrachi on Bond Street, one of a handful of designers I usually go to when I'm looking for a spectacular dress for a black-tie event. I was actually a couple of months pregnant with Princess at the time, although we hadn't announced it yet. This was the night I met Paris Hilton for the first time – she took a snap of us both together on her camera phone – and we've been friends ever since.

Meeting the Queen

I was heavily pregnant with Princess when we met the Queen on her visit to Moorfields Eye Hospital in London, where Harvey has received treatment. As I was nearing the end of the pregnancy I didn't think there was any point in buying a whole new outfit, so at the last minute our stylist at the time picked out this brown spotty dress for me. I suppose that it was suitable for the occasion, in that it was knee-length and didn't show off too much cleavage, but honestly, have you ever seen such a vile dress? Even the kids look vile.

OOPS, I DID IT AGAIN

Wherever there's a red carpet there will be paparazzi – and you can bet they'll be on the lookout for any celebrity wardrobe malfunctions. You know the sort of thing: photos of some starlet with her cellulite on show or with fake tan stains all over her hands. I've been pretty lucky in that respect – and anyway, I don't have cellulite and my tan comes from a sunbed not a bottle – but I have had a nipple accidentally pop out on a couple of occasions, most recently when I was doing the press call for my autobiography Pushed to the Limit. I was wearing a superhero-style outfit with a red and white corset, and when I put my hands over my head to pose – oops! – I ended up showing off rather more than I had intended. It was made out to be a big deal in the press and some people even accused me of doing it on purpose but really it was all very innocent. It certainly didn't bother me; it's not like people haven't seen them

before! No, if I'm ever feeling self-conscious in front of the cameras, the only person who'll know about it will be me.

Earlier this year I was lucky enough to be invited to Elton John's Oscar night party in Los Angeles. It was set to be a strictly A-list event, so I wanted to look my best and was thrilled with the stunning red dress I was having flown over to LA from Doly in London. But with just twenty-four hours to go before the big day, my dream dress was being held at airport customs with no sign that it would be released in time. I had one afternoon to find a gown for the glitziest night in Hollywood's showbiz calendar. So my manager got hold of a stylist and she took me to see a designer called Lloyd Klein, where I found a gorgeous black number: low-cut at the back and sweeping into a stunning train. It was perfect, all except for the cut at the side, which showed off too much of my boobs. It wasn't the sort of event where I was happy to have everything hanging out, so they pinned some fabric over the side and promised to alter it that way. Brilliant, I thought.

Getting ready for the Oscars. I even had lunch in these curlers

So the following evening, after I'd had my make-up done and hair styled, I took the dress out of its layers of pink tissue paper and with a little shiver of excitement slipped it on. But when I looked in the mirror it was clear that it was gaping at the side even worse than ever. They had altered it completely differently to how I had asked, and with just fifteen minutes before the car arrived to take us to the party there was nothing that could be done: I would just have to wear it like that. I was so pissed off. Everyone kept telling me how gorgeous I looked, but the whole night I was really conscious of the fact that my boob was hanging out. While I might come across as this mouthy bird, I'm really quite shy and being unhappy with the way I looked did nothing to help my self-confidence in that roomful of movie stars and Hollywood big-wigs. I just didn't feel comfortable and I swore never to use that designer again.

LIGHTS, CAMERA, ACTION!

There is a completely different set of style rules for looking good on television. Things tend to look very different under strong studio lights and through the  lens of a TV camera from the way they do in real life. But I've been doing telly for years now and have learnt from experience how to present yourself in front of the camera. For a start, I'll tailor my outfit to suit the type of show I'm appearing on. If I'm doing a daytime show like This Morning or GMTV, I'll go for brightly coloured clothes and light, pretty make-up, whereas if it's something serious I'll go for a more minimal look. Earlier this year I was interviewed by Piers Morgan for his talk show. With the dim lighting and stark set it was like being on Mastermind! So I wore a black ruffled top and leggings with thigh-length boots and wore my hair slicked back – I wanted to look like I was ready for the interrogation.

OK, so you might not have an appearance on Jonathan Ross lined up,

Before being grilled by Piers

but these days we're all caught on camera at some point, whether your mate is filming you on her mobile or you have to do a video presentation for work, so it's useful to know the essentials of putting together an on-air look. Here are my dos and don'ts…

⭐ When you're doing a TV interview you will usually only be seen from your boobs upwards, so do wear something with an interesting neckline: a pretty collar or some ruffled bits.

⭐ If you're wearing a halterneck or low-cut top, do apply a shimmer cream on your shoulders or collarbones for a flattering shine.

⭐ Don't have your tits right out. It's not a good look. And yes, I know I have been guilty of this in the past…

⭐ A striking necklace or killer earrings can look stunning, but don't wear jewellery that rattles or jangles – the microphones will pick up the slightest noise – or anything that's so shiny it will reflect the studio lights and dazzle the viewers.

⭐ Don't wear stripes, checks or zigzags. They appear to vibrate or 'strobe' when they're on camera and will make you difficult to look at.

⭐ You know you're going to be sitting down, so you don't want to be wearing a tiny skirt in case you reveal more than you intended. Also, your legs might be crossed and if you have cellulite or dimples they will be on show for everyone to see.

Put them away Kate! These days that zip wouldn't be quite so low

BEG, BORROW OR STEAL

People often don't realise that, when you see a celebrity posing away on the red carpet, chances are the glamorous outfit they're wearing doesn't actually belong to them. At the end of the night it will probably be going straight back to the designer, but if they've spilt red wine down it or ripped the hem, they'll have to pay for it. So when you see actresses or girl bands all done up in the latest designer gear and think, Wow, how incredible to have all that money to spend on clothes, just remember it is all an illusion. Half the time these people don't have the money you think they do.

The way it works is that a celebrity's stylist will call up a designer or shop's press office and say 'So-and-so is going to the Brits next week. Could you lend her an outfit?' They'll probably get sent a selection of stuff from several different places for their client to pick from, including shoes, accessories and jewellery. Then on the night, when the celebrity is going down the red carpet and a journalist asks where the dress is from, they can say, 'Prada' or 'New Look' or whatever. So it's a win–win situation: the celeb doesn't have to shell out for a frock, while the designer gets a nice bit of free advertising.

It's not that I can't afford it, but I refuse to pay twelve grand for a dress that I can only wear once because I'll have been pictured everywhere in it, so like other celebrities I like to borrow outfits for big events. You'd think with the amount of coverage I get in the magazines and papers each week designers would be more than happy to lend me an outfit, but no, I can't get any of the big names to lend to me – and it really pisses me off. The only people who regularly send me stuff are Isabell Kristensen, Anouska G and Doly by Dany Mizrachi, or up-and-coming

This was my look for appearing on the Graham Norton Show

This dress is from Doly, one of my favourite shops for gorgeous gowns

young designers like Kate Fearnley. I can almost guarantee that if my stylist phones up the likes of Versace or Gucci and asks if I can borrow an outfit for a big event they'll say, 'Sorry, all the dresses in our press office are on loan', or 'She's not the kind of person who we want wearing our clothes'. I get that all the time; it's so frustrating. I do understand why they might not have wanted me in their stuff years ago when I was out partying the whole time, as Chinawhite at 3 a.m. probably wasn't the best place for their clothes to be seen in, but now I'm probably more successful than most girls in the public eye. I look at people like Kelly Brook and I just can't understand how she gets to wear all these designer clothes. I'm not slating her, but really, what the hell does she actually do? I just wish one of the top names, someone like Roberto Cavalli whose stuff suits me really well, would have the balls to turn round and say, 'You

Pretty Woman challenge! And just to keep things fair, I decided to call up ten high-street names too to see what they would say. The results make for interesting reading…

DESIGNERS

Chanel – didn't hear back
Gucci – no response
Prada – wouldn't lend
Versace – no response
Dior – no answer
Dolce & Gabbana – didn't hear back
Roberto Cavalli – not prepared to lend
Vivienne Westwood – no answer
John Galliano – blanked me – charming!
Louis Vuitton – 'Someone will be in touch' but of course they never were
Alexander McQueen – no reply
Stella McCartney – you've guessed it… no reply

HIGH STREET

New Look, Topshop, All Saints, Miss Selfridge, River Island, H&M, Arrogant Cat, Zara, Mango and Oasis **all** said yes.

know what, Katie would look really good in one of my dresses' and give me that chance to wear it on the red carpet.

So when I started writing this book, I thought I'd put the big fashion houses to the test. I've always wanted to wear a dress by the likes of Chanel, so I decided to make it my goal to get a top designer to lend me a dress for the shoot. Yes, it's Pricey's

So although all the high-street names were happy to lend me an outfit, none of the designers would even consider doing so. I reckon it's just comes down to snobbery – pure and simple. I've proved that I can sell things, I'm credible and that people are interested in what I wear, so why won't they lend me a bloody dress? And anyway, I ended up having the last laugh because we just went to boutiques who stocked the big designers and they sent us the clothes but I didn't want to wear them anyway because some of it was vile!

5

Sex Kitten

I might have become famous for having this sexy bad-girl image, but I don't really think I naturally ooze sex appeal. Oh, I can certainly turn it on when I need to (my naughty nurse's outfit works a treat every time) but far from being a man-eater, I'm actually quite old-fashioned.

I have always made a guy wait for a minimum of one month before letting them get me into bed – and only then if we've been spending all our time together and we've got to know each other really well. It might be frustrating to wait, but in the end a bloke will respect you far more and the sex will be even hotter, so I've made that my golden rule and have pretty much always stuck to it. (OK, so I did make an exception for Pete but I ended up marrying him so that one doesn't count!)

You don't have to show all your bits to look sexy, I love this kind of girlie look

I do admit, though, before I got married, I was a bit of a prick tease. If a guy who I'd just started seeing was coming round for the evening to watch a DVD I'd make sure I got his interest by the end of the night. I'd get all dressed up in long socks with little shorts – really sexy and girlie, but not obviously trying too hard – so they'd be thinking, Mmm, she's really cute… Meanwhile I'd be thinking, Dream on, mate, you're getting none of that! These days I don't make half as much effort if I'm having a cosy night. Usually

I'll just wear a tracksuit or pyjamas – once we're at that stage of the relationship, comfort beats sex appeal hands down.

I think that some people are just naturally sexy, like the American actress Megan Fox. Not only has she got a pretty face and stunning figure, but she's obviously really confident in the way she carries herself too. If you feel good about the way you look then that will show in your aura and other people will pick up on it. I can wear a tracksuit and feel sexy as long as I know that I'm clean and well groomed.

Of course, clothes can play a big part in someone's sex appeal too. I don't really rate Jennifer Lopez's usual everyday look, but in her 'Jenny from the Block' video – wow! That's not to say that the more flesh you show, the hotter you'll look. To me, dressing

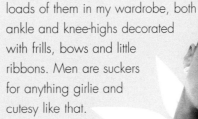

sexily isn't about red lace crotchless knickers and fishnet stockings (yuck, far too tacky top-shelf-mag for me) it's about being cute, girlie and in touch with your feminine side. A bra with pretty straps and matching boy-shorts, a hairband with a little bow, a pair of baggy hipster jeans showing a bit of toned tummy: to me all of those are really sexy. If you've got good legs I actually think pretty socks can be one of the sexiest things a woman can wear; I've got loads of them in my wardrobe, both ankle and knee-highs decorated with frills, bows and little ribbons. Men are suckers for anything girlie and cutesy like that.

ON THE PULL

I've never been very good at being chatted up. My friends used to take the piss out of me whenever blokes came up to me in clubs after I'd had a few vodkas, as I'd be all mouthy and aggressive – especially if I liked them. Some poor guy would be trying his best to talk to me and I'd be straight on the defensive: 'Look, I've got my own money, OK? I don't need you for your money. And why are you interested in me anyway? I've got a kid you know.' I think I used to be a bit scary. It was either that or I'd completely ignore them.

Dressing to attract blokes isn't rocket science. Let's face it, if you go out with your tits and legs on show then of course you're going to get male attention, so if you want to get laid then go slutty. I do sometimes look at girls in nightclubs and think, God, what a tart, but then I'll think, Kate, you're wearing the exact same thing. The crucial difference is, however, that I don't actually ever behave like a slut!

But if you're looking for boyfriend material then having it all

hanging out is clearly going to give off the wrong impression and attract the type of men who are only after one thing. In my experience, a look that most men find sexy but classy is a clingy top or skintight dress that clearly shows off the shape of your body but doesn't reveal too much flesh. Team a slinky figure-hugging outfit with a pair of high heels (an absolute essential) and you'll be turning heads for all the right reasons. Personally I don't wear tight roll-necks as I think they make me look fat because of my boobs, but men tend to love that sort of thing because they cover everything up while still hinting at what's underneath. Past boyfriends have certainly preferred me to dress in that kind of sexy, womanly style. I think if I had given them the option to put me in anything, it would be a tight pair of jeans (classier than my usual trackies because they show off my figure apparently), a nice pair of boots and a cream woolly jumper, whereas I reckon that lot would just make me look like Liz Hurley going for a country pub lunch!

THINGS MEN DEFINITELY DON'T FIND SEXY

♥ Bra straps that were once white but are now grey. It just looks dirty, and not in a good way.
♥ Visible panty line.
♥ G-strings peeking out over the back of your jeans. In fact I don't think men like G-strings full stop unless you've got a bum like Giselle.
♥ Ballet pumps. Men think they look a bit prim. I've got a lovely pair of gold Louis Vuitton pumps but Pete reckoned they were vile.
♥ Muffin top. There's no excuse for overhang; either buy a pair of jeans that fit or wear a longer T-shirt.
♥ Smock tops. Not the best thing for showing off your figure. In fact you might as well wear a tent.
♥ Ugg boots. I love mine to bits, but they're one of those things that men just don't seem to get.

FIRST DATE

You going to laugh at me, but I've never been on a date. Honestly, no man has ever taken me to dinner during those exciting, getting-to-know-you weeks of a new relationship. Whenever I've started seeing a bloke in the past, I would usually arrange to meet him in a bar or a club and would always drag a mate or two along for moral support, so then we'd all get drunk together. It would rarely be just me and him on our own until we'd been seeing each other for a good few weeks. I don't actually think I could handle going to dinner on a first date anyway. I would be so worried about making the right impression that I wouldn't be able to eat anything and then I'd probably end up having a panic attack. Pathetic!

If I did start seeing a new man my style would never be overly slutty or showy; I wouldn't want him to think I was making a special effort, as I always

liked to play it cool in the early days. Shops which are perfect for that kind of casual but sexy look are All Saints and Arrogant Cat. These days when I'm going out to dinner I'll wear something short and revealing but nothing too over-the-top outrageous. After all, you'd look a bit of a berk in a restaurant wearing PVC chaps...

LINGERIE

When it comes to lingerie, I go for girlie, feminine styles in pretty shades like pink, baby blue, turquoise, lemon and mint. But although I have drawers and drawers of lingerie in every colour of the rainbow, most of the time I end up wearing my own Katie Price

I much prefer lingerie in pretty pastels

the dance floor in front of some bloke I was trying to impress.

Wherever possible I always try to wear the coordinating knickers to whatever bra I've got on, as it's important to me that every element of my outfit matches. I think boy-shorts are far more flattering than thongs, but I will usually wear a string brief with a clingy outfit to avoid visible panty line.

In my experience, high-street lingerie brands are just as good as high-end designer ranges. Who has time to hand-wash pricey silk knickers anyway? When I'm out shopping, rather than looking at the label I will always go for how pretty bras look and how well

underwear range. It's been tailor-made for me so it fits absolutely perfectly, plus I've designed the bra straps to be pretty enough to have peeking out under a vest top or sheer T-shirt. There are a few exceptions, though. If I'm wearing a tracksuit top or something more covered-up I'll usually go for a sports bra, as it's the most comfortable option and gives my boobs extra support, while for a really killer cleavage on nights out I tend to put on a Wonderbra. Obviously I don't need to wear any extra padding these days, but before I had implants I used to stuff shoulder pads down the front of my bra to give me a bit of a boost. Even if chicken fillets had been around when I was a flat-chested teenager, I don't think I'd have worn them as I'd have been terrified that one of them would suddenly flop out on

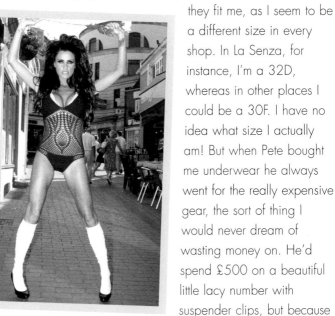

they fit me, as I seem to be a different size in every shop. In La Senza, for instance, I'm a 32D, whereas in other places I could be a 30F. I have no idea what size I actually am! But when Pete bought me underwear he always went for the really expensive gear, the sort of thing I would never dream of wasting money on. He'd spend £500 on a beautiful little lacy number with suspender clips, but because it cost so much I felt I should save it for a special occasion and then I never ended up wearing it.

When it comes to the bedroom, I much prefer sexy uniforms – police or nurse outfits that I get from sex shops – to the black and red lacy basques, stockings and suspenders that some men seem to think look sexy. That's all a bit 1980s glamour model for my liking. I do have that sort of thing in pretty, girlie colours, but I'll usually have the suspender clips hanging loose and not bother with stockings, and I'll only ever wear it in the bedroom. As for what I wear to sleep in bed, I'm sorry to shatter any illusions but it's usually just a well-supported sports bra and nothing else. Pretty sexy, eh?

I'm Katie, come fly me!

Black suspenders, stockings and basque – not the kind of thing I like to wear

MEN'S STYLE

As far as I'm concerned, the sexiest style on a man is what I call the pretty-boy gay look: immaculately groomed and in touch with his feminine side, as seen on most boy-band members and gay men. It's important for me that my man makes an effort with his appearance, which means being well turned out, looking clean and smelling good. I think the footballer Christiano Ronaldo has the perfect pretty-boy style, although you'd have to chop off his head as I'm not so keen on that face! And I love a guy who looks particularly great in a tight pair of Calvin Klein boxers which show off his fantastic arse. I always make sure Harvey and Junior are dressed trendily too; in fact, Pete sometimes nicks some of Harvey's clothes. A while ago, I bought Harvey some really nice gear from All Saints and I quickly noticed that it had somehow found its way into Pete's wardrobe!

I quite like a man in a suit and I don't even mind an edgier rocker look (as long as it's all spotlessly clean – sweaty leather kecks are a definite no-no) but I really can't stand grunge or goth. I see someone who's all pale, dressed head to toe in grungy black layers, and just think, You look like you need a good bath, mate.

When it comes to grooming, I reckon most British blokes just don't make enough effort. The things I always notice on a man are whether they've got neat nails, a good haircut and white teeth. I don't even mind if men wear a bit of make-up, as long as it's done discreetly. Pete once wore a touch of smoky eyeliner when we performed at the club night G-A-Y in London, and it looked really sexy. As for body hair, personally I prefer my man to be completely clean-shaven. One of my first boyfriends before I was famous, Gary, had a proper chest rug and I didn't mind it at the time, although these days I'd

probably get him to whip it all off. But a full back, sack and crack is an absolute, 100 per cent must. Why is it that some blokes expect their girlfriends to be completely bald down below, but they don't bother to sort out their own? As far as I'm concerned, a bloke's bits have got to be neatly trimmed, because let's be honest – who wants a mouthful of hair? And another thing which is completely non-negotiable for me when it comes to male grooming is feet. I can think of few things more disgusting than what the average British male has lurking under his socks. Hideous yellowing toenails and flaky skin is an instant and total turn-off.

MATCHING UP TO YOUR MAN

If I'm going to an event with my bloke we will almost always make an effort to match our outfits, like here at the Disney Channel Kids Awards with Pete in 2004. I've always got a picture of how we'll look together in the back of my mind, so whether it's the colour or style of clothes we try to have an element of our outfits that coordinates as I believe it makes for a far better photo. I don't think that's just true for celebrities either, I love to see a couple who've obviously made an effort to think about how they'll look next to each other. I occasionally involve the kids too – sometimes we'll all wear the same colour, like different shades of cream, but other times we'll all be in all different colours, like a rainbow. We're lucky in that we've got such a wide choice of clothes so can all match up quite easily, but I do appreciate that most families probably can't afford to do that.

6

Entrepreneur

In business, my ambition is nothing less than global domination. I might have started with Britain, but in the next few years I plan to launch my products all over the world. As far as I'm concerned, the sky's the limit. (Actually, I'm not even sure that's the case – what do you think about a Katie Price airline?) I want to be known as the girl who came from nothing and went on to conquer the world.

I love it when people tell me I can't do something, or that it will never work, because getting knocked back is what motivates me. When I first started my modelling career, a skinny teenager with no boobs and curly brunette hair, I struggled to get people to take me seriously and would have the door shut in my face time and time again. The glamour models of the day were all blonde with big fake tits, so I'd go on castings and

The kids sometimes come along to my launches to help out

people would tell me I was too short or just not the right look. But in those days, just as now, the more I got turned down, the more determined and driven I became. It's the best feeling in the world when you prove the doubters wrong. Now my perfumes, hair products, bedding, pyjamas, swimwear, jewellery, equestrian range and lingerie are all best-sellers – and I've lots more products to come.

For me, success is more about power than money, but I can't deny that I've done well out of my business deals over the years. In terms of how much I've earned there have been all sorts of figures thrown around (most of them pretty wide of the mark!) but I couldn't have achieved everything I have and worked as hard as I do

My brother Danny keeps a tight hold of the purse

without making quite a bit of money along the way. I like to keep my financial matters in the family so my brother Danny, who's got a degree in business, looks after my money and is constantly on my case and telling me to stop spending, so even though I'm comfortably off and have a nice house and cars I actually live quite modestly. But I don't have a mortgage or owe anything on credit. A lot of my friends have less money in the bank and they have far more glamorous, extravagant lives. But just because I don't flaunt it, it doesn't mean I don't have it.

For one launch I used members of my fan club as models but this time I invited my mates along – even my mum got her kit off!

So does money give you happiness? No, money gives you material things. It means that I can get my nails done three times a week and keep my horses, and it gives my family security. But I've lived without money before and I have no doubt that if I lost everything I could do again. I'm pretty well grounded; it honestly wouldn't matter to me if I had to move to a smaller house. As long as the kids were safe and happy, I'd be fine.

I'm often asked why I've been so successful in business. I think it comes down to hard work and staying true to myself. Loads of celebrities just put their name to a product, get paid a nice fat endorsement fee and then have nothing more to do with it, but that's not the way I do things. Before starting something new I always want to know what people are trying to achieve from a project long-term, as I've no interest in working with anyone who's just trying to turn a fast buck. I always set out my goals and then work out how I am going to achieve them. I believe that if you're going to promote a product you should be prepared to put everything behind it, which is why you'll see me standing in front of the paparazzi wearing my lingerie range, rather than sticking it on a load of skinny models and just posing next to them like other celebrities I could mention. I'll only take on a business project if I'm 100 per cent involved at every stage because for me the fun part is the creative process, and I would never enter into a deal if I wasn't convinced it would be successful. Failure is something I'd never waste time even considering.

As much as I'm ambitious and determined to get results, when I start work on a new project I never go into it feeling the need to prove myself. In business, it's important to have a sense of self-worth because if you don't believe in yourself, how can you expect others to? So when I go into meetings my attitude is this: you're either interested or you're not, and if you're not I'll just take it somewhere else – I'm not going to beg.

Whatever work you do though, one of the best pieces of advice I can give you is that you'll get better results if you keep things fun. In meetings I'll always make sure I get my point across, but then I'll have a laugh and make sure everyone else does too. Most of our lives are spent working, so I think it's really important that you find a job you enjoy. What's that expression? Do what you love and the money will follow.

I don't have a suit in my wardrobe but I thought it'd be fun to try one on for the book. Do I look like I mean business?

DRESSED FOR SUCCESS

I've never owned a suit. My kind of business wear is more likely to be a silver sequinned catsuit and matching feathered bolero with platform heels. If I do have a meeting, I'll just turn up in whatever I am wearing that day. People can take me as I am, which is usually with my hair scraped back in a ponytail, no make-up, a tracksuit and Uggs. I don't think you should use your looks to help you get ahead in business – unless you work as an escort, of course! But even if I'm casually dressed I'll always make sure I'm immaculately groomed. First impressions are important and in meetings the first thing I notice about

about capturing the public's interest. It's about getting as many people as possible to see that picture of me wearing my nightwear range or showing off my hair straighteners. For instance, I chose the name Angel for my first novel because I knew I wanted to wear big fluffy white wings at the press launch, and I called my second perfume Besotted because I had this vision of me looking really romantic and love-struck, like I was on a moonlit beach with some gorgeous hunk. So you see, what I wear is key to a project's success and I absolutely love thinking up more and more outrageous concepts for press calls to ensure I get my products out there. I'm even thinking of going stark naked for my next autobiography launch, so watch this space!

This is my usual sort of business attire.

other women is whether their hair and nails look neat and their clothes are ironed. If someone turned up in a crumpled shirt and bitten nails I'd struggle to take them seriously.

In the case of my product and book launches, however, what I wear is absolutely crucial. In fact, I choose the names of all my projects purely on what outfit I'm going to wear for the press call because at the end of the day my business is all

If I did have to dress up for a business meeting, this is the sort of look I'd go for

Unless I'm promoting one of my own clothing ranges, like my lingerie or equestrian lines, all my press call outfits are made at a theatrical costumiers in London who are brilliant at turning my crazy ideas into reality. They know my sizes, so all I have to do is phone up and tell them the sort of thing I want then they'll put together some sketches and send them over for me to add or change details if necessary; I'm really hands-on throughout the whole process. The finished

I used this outfit but bloody hell, it was tight around my bits

outfit will then be fitted on me, to make sure everything is perfect. Occasionally there will be a small problem (on the day of the press launch for my novel Angel Uncovered I discovered that the silver catsuit I was wearing was way too tight around my wotsit – you can see me smiling through gritted teeth in the photos!) but usually it's a very smooth process and surprisingly speedy too. It usually takes about ten days from my initial phone call to the completed outfit, but they can have it done in less. I reckon they push me to the top of the list because I'm such a good customer.

It's hard for me to say which has been my favourite press call outfit because I've loved them all for different reasons, but I suppose I'm happiest when I can get my kit off. People don't realise what a massive adrenaline buzz it is to stand in front of all those photographers virtually starkers. Other people might get nightmares about appearing naked in public, but personally I get a great big kick out of it! It's like a secret challenge to myself: it doesn't matter whether I've got my boobs, legs, bum or belly on show, when those pictures appear in the newspapers the next day they're not going to be airbrushed. It's as raw as it can possibly be.

I've been doing press calls for years now, so I know exactly how to ensure all the photographers get a good shot of me. As soon as I walk out in front of the rows of paparazzi they'll all be shouting for me to look their way and the camera flashes will be blinding. But I'll just be calmly thinking, Look to the right, left, up, down, so everyone gets some eye contact, and then I'll change the pose and do it all over again. When it comes to my job I'm a perfectionist and I know I'm good at what I do.

Modelling is a skill, and it makes me so frustrated when I see actresses doing photo shoots who clearly have no idea how to pose and end up looking completely uncomfortable and unnatural. OK, there's always going to be a camera that catches me at an unflattering angle, but as long as people are writing about my product I'm not that bothered what I look like in the photos. I love proving to people that I am real (well, bits of me anyway) and that what you see in the press is actually what I look like. Don't get me wrong, for magazine shoots I like a bit of airbrushing as much as the next celebrity, but for events like my lingerie launch I think it's important that people see how the product looks on a real woman.

MY FAVOURITE LAUNCH OUTFITS

Electrical hair products

1 With my electrical hair range I wanted to be able to show off the products during the launch, so I told the costume designers that I'd be having half my hair straight and the other half tonged into curls and needed an outfit to reflect that. Plus, the products are pink and white so I wanted to continue that colour theme. This is what they came up with — and I loved it.

KP Equestrian

2 I think people imagined I'd be standing there in jodhpurs and boots when I did my first equestrian launch, which is why I decided to do something totally different. You've got to give journalists stuff that's eye-catching enough to be worth printing. So I dreamed up a Barbie-style set with an almost cartoonish feel and wore pink hot pants with long socks and painted the horse's hooves to match my outfit. It worked so well that I'm actually planning a range of nail varnish for horses.

Crystal

3 When you're a week away from giving birth (as I was here) there isn't really much you can wear and look good. So for my book launch at Harrods I decided to go completely over the top with a big fluffy meringue of a dress, a sparkly crown and a handful of half-naked men to carry my fairytale carriage. I'm never happy with how I look when I'm pregnant, but I loved the princess theme, I felt comfortable and I think I looked the best I possibly could in the circumstances.

7

Beach Babe

These days it's rare that I get to go somewhere hot and sunny without a camera crew trailing around after me, but I do my best to make sure that I have two completely work-free holidays a year to give myself a chance to properly chill out, relax – and do lots of naked sunbathing! My ideal destination is somewhere extremely remote and very, very hot, where the only people I'd see throughout my whole stay would be the kids, a masseuse or

Waiting at the airport to jet off on a girlie holiday.

My mum with Harvey on holiday.

beauty therapist and possibly a butler to bring me ice-cold daiquiris: the whole desert-island fantasy, but with six-star luxury facilities. My best ever holiday was a two-week trip to the Maldives before I got married. We just hung out in our gorgeous water villa with its glass floor, through which you could see the Indian Ocean and an occasional tropical fish. Bliss. I went back there for my honeymoon and again when I split

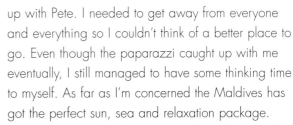

up with Pete. I needed to get away from everyone and everything so I couldn't think of a better place to go. Even though the paparazzi caught up with me eventually, I still managed to have some thinking time to myself. As far as I'm concerned the Maldives has got the perfect sun, sea and relaxation package.

As much as I love lazing around on a beach all day, I do enjoy different types of holiday too. I always have a great time when I go away with my mates to Ibiza. We'll hire a gorgeous villa and then just chill out, have a laugh and party. I'm not really a proper clubber (well, not these days!) but it's a great place to have a few big nights out in between all the sunbathing. Having said that, I did have the worst holiday of my life in Ibiza back when I was about 19. I went to San Antonio with some mates and we stayed in the most awful hotel you can imagine. It was dirty and noisy, the food was terrible and everything about the resort was crap. I couldn't wait to get home.

As I'm quite sporty I'd also love to have a go at skiing one day, but I'd have to wrap up in loads of layers of warm clothes as I can't stand being cold – which is the reason that I've never tried it before. I would need to have a serious shopping spree before hitting the slopes…

PACKING

People always take the piss out of me for taking far too much stuff when I go on holiday and taking too long to pack, but I've tried to limit myself to a capsule wardrobe before (where you take just a few items that you mix and match, like doubling up your sarong as a halter-neck dress for the evening) and it has never worked. I get to the hotel, open my suitcase and think, I don't want to wear any of that – I knew I should've brought more stuff. Wherever I'm going though, the two essentials I will always have in my bag will be a tracksuit (yes, even in the Maldives – it can get quite cold in the evening) and a tooth-brush and toothpaste. I could survive anywhere with those.

I'm extremely organised when it comes to my holiday packing. First of all I'll work out how many days and nights I'm going for – let's say it's a week-long trip. So I will take seven daytime outfits for hot weather, seven daytime outfits for not-so-hot weather (you never know if it's going to rain), seven beach outfits and seven night-time outfits. So that's four outfits a day, which makes a grand total of… twenty-eight outfits for a week. I will then go through my wardrobes and carefully plan each look right down to the underwear to make sure it all matches up

perfectly. I'll pull out a pair of knickers, bra, shoes, socks, earrings, bracelet, hairclips, vest top, trousers and bags and put it in a little pile, or for the beach option a bikini, sarong, hat, flip-flops, necklace and hairband. Now can you see why I end up taking so much stuff? I'll end up with twenty-eight heaps of clothes, shoes and accessories all over the bed and spilling onto the floor. Once I've planned all my outfits and packed up my expensive creams, lotions and hair products (most of which I won't use) I fold all the clothes up as small as they'll go to make sure I can get loads into one bag. Most of my clothes are so tiny they pack up into nothing anyway, and I hardly ever buy anything that needs ironing (linen is definitely out of the question) so my outfits will be crumple-free and ready to wear when I arrive.

It's a brilliant system; well, it would be if I actually wore the outfits that I planned, but more often than not I'll end up in the same bikini top and trackie bottoms for most of my stay. I don't really know why I take so much beachwear, as I prefer to sunbathe nude, and usually end up having dinner in the villa rather than at a restaurant so I don't really need all the evening options either. Still, at least I know that I'm fully prepared for any occasion!

A WORD ABOUT SUITCASES...

When you're choosing luggage, my advice would be to take the cheapest, plainest and most understated that you can find. I might like to stand out from the crowd, but when it comes to my suitcases the opposite is definitely true. I've had all the Guccis and Louis Vuittons, but I began to realise that my expensive bags were always the ones that mysteriously went missing during the flight. In my experience, the more luxury and appealing your suitcase, the more

Our luggage for LA, not a designer brand in sight

likely it is that it will be nicked or someone will have a root through it then claim it's been damaged in transit. A cheap suitcase won't look so inviting and is more likely to arrive at your destination safely and in one piece. Hand luggage is different, as you'll have it with you the whole time so you can go as glam as you like, but my advice would be to always go cheap for check-in.

Over the years I've had countless suitcases that have been 'lost' and have never once got my stuff back. I

remember one time I had a charity job in a poor part of India. I arrived to find my suitcase had split and everything had vanished, so I didn't have anything to wear for the job, no make-up, toiletries – nothing. As there were no shops I had to spend the whole three days of our trip in what I had been wearing on the plane. That was pretty shit, I can tell you.

FLYING

If I'm going on holiday, I normally like to dress up a bit for the airport. Definitely not to impress the paparazzi, but because I've always felt that there's something sort of glamorous about jetting off somewhere exotic – and as I know I won't be lugging lots of stuff about it doesn't matter how high my heels are. So I'll usually go for jeans and a nice jacket, and if it's a long-haul flight – eight hours plus – I'll take a pair of pyjamas in my hand luggage to change into on the plane so I can get really comfy. It's a different matter if I'm flying somewhere for work though. If I'm getting a flight to a signing or promotional event I will usually have to change into something dressier, shorter and more revealing when I arrive, so I'll always go for a baggy tracksuit and Ugg boots on the plane as leggings or skinny jeans can leave a crease imprinted on your legs that takes ages to fade.

I'm not a nervous flyer, but I do find it extremely boring being stuck on a plane for hours – unless the kids are with me, in which case it's just bloody stressful. So to pass the time if I'm on my own, I sleep. I usually start off by flicking through a magazine, but then I'll quickly drop off; I don't need an eye mask or ear plugs, I've always been very good at just curling up in a ball and within minutes I'll be out. Usually I'll be lucky enough to be flying First or Business Class, so it's a bit easier to get comfy than it is in Economy.

*Glamming it up
at the airport*

I do always eat whatever food I'm offered when I'm flying as boredom makes me even hungrier, but I never find the tiny portions they give you are big enough to fill me up, so I always ask for two of each meal.

If I'm wearing make-up when I get on the plane, I take it off with my MAC wipes and slather on loads of moisturiser during the flight, as I find your skin can really dry out. Then before I leave the plane I'll just stick on a pair of huge sunglasses and a bit of lip gloss so I don't have to worry about looking crappy and knackered if there are paparazzi lurking around the airport.

WHAT'S IN MY INFLIGHT BAG

Money
Passport
Magazine
Laptop
Make-up wipes
Lip gloss
Moisturiser
Pyjamas (if I'm going long-haul)
Sunglasses

My anti-paparazzi shades

BEACH

When I go on holiday I like to do as little as possible. My days usually go like this: get up late, eat breakfast, sunbathe, eat lunch, sunbathe, have a dip in the sea, sunbathe, go for a spa treatment or massage, eat dinner, sleep. I'll usually stick to my private villa, so I don't have to worry about being overlooked by other people, and I'll put music on in the background while I completely chill out. In the evening I'll watch DVDs, play Scrabble or card games like gin rummy. These days I usually take a book with me on holiday too. I prefer true crime, thrillers or stuff about serial killers – anything fucked up! The last one I read was about people on death row: what crimes they committed, their last meal and last words. Personally, my death row meal would be chicken kiev, sweetcorn and chips. And my last words? Fuck you all. Well, I am about to be marched off to the electric chair!

On Safari, not my usual kind of hoilday but I loved it all the same

Being seen in a swimming hat was less embarassing than being seen without my hair extensions

shape. The triangle tops suit both small and large boobs (unless yours are really droopy) and the adjustable bottoms mean you don't have to worry about getting a muffin top. Unless I'm sunbathing naked, I like to wear the smallest size of bikini I can get away with because I hate having tan lines, but I'm not so keen on the look of thongs so I usually go for a Brazilian cut brief, which offers a bit more coverage. I usually get my bikinis at the Kings Road Sporting Club in London, Beach Bunny (an American brand you can get online) or in boutiques in America, but wherever I am if something catches my eye I'll get it. When we were in the Maldives I bought all these gorgeous, very expensive bikinis which I then forgot to pack. They're probably still sitting in the hotel room drawer!

I can happily spend all day sunbathing. I know this is terrible, but I don't usually wear any sort of sun protection when I'm lying out as my skin is so used to being tanned from going on the sunbed every day that I don't seem to need it. I do use suntan lotion, but it's the Hawaiian Tropic oil which doesn't give any SPF protection, unless I've burnt my face in which case I'll use something with a UV filter to stop my eyes getting sore and puffy. Sunburn completely ruins your holiday.

I don't usually wear a swimming hat, although I did have to once on our TV show as I didn't have my hair extensions in and I hate people seeing me without them. But if I've been in the sea I might put leave-in conditioner in my hair while I'm sunbathing to protect it.

By the way, I've never understood why some women wear a full face of make-up to the beach. Surely you'd just sweat it all off in a few minutes anyway?

When it comes to bikinis, I think the string variety is by far the most flattering option for every body

String bikinis are very flattering

One piece swimsuits can look great but I only wear them for shoots

I do like the look of one-piece swimsuits, especially the ones with sexy cut-outs and mesh detailing, but I can't wear them as I'm a bit too short in the body and they tend to go saggy round my belly. As for men's swimwear, give me a sexy pair of baggy board shorts over Speedos any day – unless a guy's got a really fit body, in which case they can just about get away with a pair of tight little briefs.

If I need to cover up during the day on holiday I'll wear a sarong or a pair of trackie bottoms. I hate anyone seeing my cellulite, so I'd never wear a tiny skirt or hot pants in the daytime, although I might wear something like that at night when it's dark enough to cover up any dimples. As for crop tops – no fucking way! Not with my belly. When you've had three kids it's definitely not the sort of thing you want to be making a feature of…

8

Girlie Girl

I have never really been sure what to write on my passport in the bit where you have to state your profession. Should I put Model? Entrepreneur? Author? Celebrity Mum of the Year 2007...? Actually, I think the most accurate answer would probably be Katie Price: Girlie Girl.

To me, being a girlie girl means making sure you're always immaculately turned out and being fully in touch with your inner Disney princess. Whenever I'm out shopping, my eye is instantly drawn to things which are pretty, pink or glittery – or preferably all three. Even my VW Beetle looks like something Barbie would drive. My daughter Princess is exactly the same: if she sees some diamante sparkling on my T-shirt or if I'm wearing pink lip gloss she'll point and go, 'Pretty, pretty!' Actually, I think 'pretty' was probably her first word.

Even though I'm a mum, I still want to look young, fun and feminine. Imagine what a Playboy bunny girl would wear to pop out for lunch with friends on her days off and that's exactly the sort of look that I love – little ra-ra skirts with long knee-socks in bright candy colours or hot pants with a cutesy cartoon T-shirt, pretty little ankle socks and matching wedges. I adore all my diamonds, but I'm really just as happy wearing a cheap necklace with a little pastel-coloured ice-cream pendant hanging off it. Even when I'm a granny I'll probably still be there sitting next to my gas

heater, all cosy in a frilly pink cardi with a matching blanket studded with pink Swarowski crystals…

Being girlie is not just about lip gloss and legwarmers though, it's about having a laugh with your best mates and not taking life too seriously. My

friends are all girlie girls too; even my gay best mates Gary and Phil are fully in touch with their feminine side! That's not to say that we're all airheads – far from it. People make the mistake of assuming that just because a girl likes to dress up and have fun with her look she's not got much going on upstairs, but there's no way I would have been as successful as I am in my career if I was some ditzy bimbo. As I've always told people, never underestimate the Pricey! I wouldn't be friends with an airhead either: my gang are all strong, successful adults with kids or careers, and we'd quickly lose patience with a dimmo.

I have a very small close-knit group of mates, nearly all of whom I've known since before I became famous and who I trust 100 per cent. I do of course have other friends who I love to meet up with when we have the time, like Michelle Heaton, Paris Hilton and Alex Curran, but as far as my BFs go there's Gary, Phil, Jamelah, Julie, Melodie and my little sister Sophie, and that's about it really. But while I might not have that many of them, the friends I do have are extremely important to me and each bring something different to my life. I love our little group because there's no bitchiness or back-stabbing and we all trust each other to tell the truth. We don't try to be better than each other, so no one's ever threatened by anyone else, and I know I can completely be myself when I'm with

them. These days it's hard for me to make new friends because I don't ever know if people want to get to know me just because I'm famous, and then I worry they might sell stories on me as it's happened so many times before. Anyway, I'm perfectly happy with the friends I've got – I just wish I had time to see them more often.

Because I'm constantly rushing around for work or with the kids I tend to keep up with my friends' news via text, unless of course there's major gossip in which case I'll be straight on the phone for the latest updates – and if I want to have a good moan to someone it'll always be my friends who get their ears chewed off too. Whenever we do manage to meet up though, it almost always revolves around food. Everyone will come over to my house and I'll cook a big roast lamb or we'll have a barbecue and then we'll all pile into our cinema room to watch reality TV or crap DVDs on the big screen. If I had the time I would love to meet up with my friends for girlie lunches or even afternoon tea at a posh hotel, as when we do make the effort to dress up and go somewhere nice, rather than just getting pissed at a nightclub, we have such a laugh. A few months ago we had a properly girlie night out. We started at the London restaurant Hakkasan, which is a really glamorous place that does amazing Chinese food and cocktails,

A girlie night out with my friend, Alex Curran

Me and Sophie hit the tiles

I love meeting up with Paris when I'm stateside

My best friends Jamelah, Gary and Phil

My pink VW Beetle

and then we all went to the theatre to see Grease. It's very rare we do something like that, but it was great fun. At the moment there's talk about going out for a day's clay pigeon shooting – I say bring it on!

When it comes to style all my friends have their own unique look, which is great because it means we're never competing with each other when we go out. My sister Sophie is quite quirky and rocky, Julie is always in a black smock dress with black tights and Melodie won't go out in anything too short, but she does love a slut dress that shows off plenty of cleavage! Gary and Phil always look immaculate. As they are both in creative careers – Gary's a make-up artist and Phil's an interior designer – they can give me a bloke's point of view about what looks good, but a bloke with really fantastic taste who understands which shoes work with which dress, rather than one who just wants to get me into bed!

My mini-me, Princess

Girlie…

…and girlier

I love charm jewellery like these ice cream pendants just as much as I love my stunning diamond earrings

Meanwhile, Jamelah has a really sexy style, but is always perfectly classy and elegant. She works as a stylist, so has a wardrobe full of amazing designer gear and I'll often borrow stuff from her.

If we're going on a night out we will usually get ready together and my friends will nearly always make some comment about what I'm wearing, especially if Jordan's come out to play! Jamelah will take one look at me and go, 'Kate, there is no way you can go out in that.' So the next thing you know I'll be marching around the house in a tiny white see-through dress and skyscraper heels to find out exactly what everyone else thinks. But it doesn't matter what anybody says, if I want to wear something, no one can talk me out of it, and so later that evening we'll be walking into the Sanderson Hotel for cocktails and I'll look like a cheap hooker in my slutty white dress. Love it!

Every true girlie girl matches her nails to her dress

SHOPPING

Like all true girlie girls, I love going shopping. I just wish I had more time to indulge my passion. What I'd really like is to have two full days where I could go to Harrods or Harvey Nicks and work my way slowly through every department to make sure I haven't missed anything. As it is, I'm so busy that I end up squeezing in a sneaky spree in between getting my nails done at the beauty salon or picking up the kids. Because of that, I usually end up going shopping on my own, but when I get the chance I do love getting dressed up in a nice pair of jeans and heels and going for a day in London with Jamelah.

My shopping style could best be described as 'smash and grab'. I'll park outside a shop, run in and quickly scan through all the rails, then if I see something I like I'll just buy it in every colour. I don't ever try anything on (unless of course I'm having something tailor-made) and I won't usually bother to check the prices of things apart from when I'm in the sort of shop where you just know there'll be a few extra zeroes added on the end, in which case I'll take a little peek and think, How much for a bloody T-shirt? They're having a laugh!

I admit that it's not the most sensible way of buying clothes, as it usually means I'll come home with bags of stuff that doesn't quite fit, or that I've already got in my wardrobe but just forgotten about. I'm particularly prone to doubling up on items when I go shopping at Abercrombie & Fitch, a great American brand which I love for tracksuits and tops. I'll grab armfuls of vest tops without even realising that I already have the exact same ones at home, and then I'll never get

coloured basics. As much as I love meeting my fans, it is quite hard trying to shop when people keep stopping you for autographs and photos, so when I'm shopping I tend not to look at anyone or give any eye contact. Most of the time it works and people leave me alone, but if someone does come up to me and tries to start talking I usually pretend I haven't heard them and that does the trick! I would love to spend more time browsing, but often I'm being followed around by the paparazzi and although they can't actually come into the shops, they hang around outside taking pictures through the window so the whole thing becomes a bit of an ordeal. They're complete scum, and I find it so annoying that I'm seriously thinking about getting into online shopping. I've never had a go at it before, but Jamelah is a pro and she's promised to get me started and show me some good websites. I have a feeling it could be quite addictive…

round to taking them back so they just sit in my wardrobes gathering dust.

When it comes to my own clothes I'm not really into designer labels, although I don't mind spending a bit extra on quality classics like a nice leather jacket or cashmere jumper that won't date. On the high street the one place I can guarantee I'll always buy something is River Island; my other favourites include All Saints, the big Topshop on Oxford Street and American Apparel, which is brilliant for brightly

I love the high street but I don't mind spending a bit more on things like leather jacketss

WHERE I SHOP FOR MY...

TRACKSUITS AND T-SHIRTS

If you say tracksuits people immediately think 'chav', but the tracksuits that I wear don't tend to be cheap, they are beautiful quality and can be quite expensive. There isn't any one particular place I go for them – if I see something and I like it, I'll buy it – but I can usually find something

I love LA boutique Kitson

at Kitson (a fab boutique in LA), Kings Road Sporting Club in London, Pineapple and American Apparel. My favourite brands include the Italian dancewear designer Deha, Juicy and E.vil, which makes those diamante-covered girlie tees and trackies you'll often see me wearing. You can get their clothes in Harrods.

T-shirt from E.vil

SHOES

My favourite shoe shops include Gina, Moda Pelle and Christian Louboutin, where I went mad when I was last in America and came back with loads of gorgeous heels. I also love Havaiana flip-flops and buy them in America where you can get them customised with diamante.

JEANS

In terms of fit and style, I don't think you can beat Frankie B jeans. I've probably got about sixty pairs, although I don't wear them that much. As a rule I prefer my clothes to look brand new and freshly washed, but I make an exception when it comes to jeans as I think a few rips can look quite sexy, especially a little one on the bum cheek. I used to customise my own with rips and then tie-dye them.

DRESSES

At the moment, I don't really go anywhere other than Doly on London's New Bond Street for dresses. They fit my body shape perfectly and the styling is really sexy – ultra-girlie and glamorous. I also like Kate Fearnley, Lipsy and Anouska G.

JEWELLERY

When I'm looking for fun costume jewellery I go to places like Butler and Wilson, Mikey and Freedom in Topshop, but for the real deal I use the jewellery designer who created my wedding ring. He used to create pieces for the Royal family, so he certainly knows his stuff! I'm a jewellery freak. I wouldn't buy a designer outfit, but I'd happily invest in a really expensive watch. The jewellery in my collection that I probably wear the most often is a pair of pear-cut diamond ear studs. When it comes to precious stones, I'll always go for diamonds over rubies, emeralds or sapphires.

WEDDINGS

I couldn't write a chapter on being a girlie girl and not include the most lavishly girlie moment of my whole life – my wedding day.

Ever since I was a little girl, I had a dream of walking down the aisle to marry my handsome prince in a sparkly pink dress with a long floaty train and a big crown – the whole fairytale princess get-up. And of course I got to live out my fantasy when I tied the knot with Pete in 2005.

It was haute couture designer Isabell Kristensen who turned my wedding dress dreams into reality – and the end result was just as show-stopping as I had imagined. The dress was three metres wide, with a

My favourite earrings and one of my designer watches

Me and my bridesmaids getting ready

skirt of pale pink satin topped with pink tulle and puffed up with layers of petticoats, with a seven-metre long satin train. To get the dazzling effect I wanted, the bodice was completely covered in thousands of rose-pink Swarovski crystals, with thousands more scattered over the tulle overskirt. Apparently it took a team of twelve seamstresses nearly a month to stitch all of the 800 sheets of crystals onto my dress by hand. To balance out the huge skirt, I wore a crown made of more rose and clear-coloured Swarovski crystals in the shape of interlocking love hearts.

The whole outfit cost hundreds of thousands of pounds, and while I was prepared to spend a lot of money on my wedding dress – which is the most important outfit of a woman's life – I have to admit I was never 100 per cent happy with that dress. It did look stunning, but it was just so bloody uncomfortable. The corset was far too short in the body, so although it was altered numerous times it never fitted me quite right and was digging into my belly all day. I was wearing three hairpieces and had my own hair pulled so tight underneath it all that my scalp started to bleed, by which time it was too late to take the pieces off and change it. It was awful! I hate to say it, but I much preferred the dress that I wore for my renewing my wedding vows three years later, a stunningly sexy white and silver number from Doly. If I had my wedding day all over again, I'd definitely go to them for the dress.

I love how I looked but my head really hurt

FINDING THE PERFECT WEDDING DRESS

♥ You only get married once (or so I hoped, I certainly never dreamed I'd be divorced) so don't be afraid to go over the top. If you've got your heart set on a baby-blue dress with a twenty-foot train then don't let anyone talk you out of it – it's your day.

♥ For me, choosing a dress was all about the wow factor; I wanted something that people would remember, rather than just another basic white gown.

♥ Remember that the back view of your dress is just as important as the front, as that's what people will see when you're standing up saying your vows.

♥ Make sure you have a trial run, trying on the dress with all the accessories and having your hair done the way you want it on the day, just to check everything works together.

♥ If you're going for a really show-stopping gown, you might want to consider wearing another outfit (perhaps a shorter, sexier version of your wedding dress – I had a pink tulle tutu made to match mine) for when the after-dinner dancing kicks off.

Renewing my wedding vows

My wedding tutu

9

Sports Star

I come from a very sporty family. My mum used to swim for England when she was in her 20s and she is still an incredible swimmer today. You should see her gliding up and down our indoor swimming pool at home; she's just like a fish – so smooth and effortless through the water. She was even supposed to be on the Olympic team alongside gold medallist Sharron Davies, but she blew it out because my dad was jealous and didn't want her to do it. They had a stormy relationship and at the time I'm sure she just wanted to keep him happy, but I know she still regrets that decision.

Because my mum was such a water baby, my brother and I got into swimming at a young age and by the age of 6 I was training for an hour three times every week, as well as doing gymnastics. I used to swim for Sussex when I was at school – butterfly was my speciality – but then in my early teens I had an accident and started to have panic attacks when I went near water. I'm much better today, although I do wonder how far I could have gone if I'd been able to keep up the swimming. But at least it meant I had more time to indulge my true sporting passion…

HORSE RIDING

My mum had no idea what she was letting herself in for when she first took me to meet her friend's ponies when I was seven. I was instantly and seriously hooked. From that moment on, I was obsessed with anything horse-related and would spend every penny of my pocket money on whatever I could find with a picture of a pony on it. When I was 11 Mum let me have a horse on loan, and four years later I finally got one of my own, an ex-racehorse named Star. But although I adored everything to do with horses and riding (it wasn't enough that my walls were covered with pony pictures; I once even smuggled a bale of hay and a horse bucket into my bedroom) I was pretty unimpressed with what the tweedy equestrian fashion world had to offer. For a young girl who was desperate to stand out, the high-waisted jodhpurs and frumpy jumpers in boring beige were dull beyond words.

Years later this early disappointment would inspire me to create my own KP Equestrian clothing range, which is full of bright candy colours and fashion-led styling – the sort of stuff I would have loved when I was a horse-mad little girl. I want to sprinkle a bit of girlie glamour over the riding world! And I don't know if I've had anything to do with it, but I do think the industry is waking up to the fact that there is a market for riding gear in more than the most basic styles and shades. The other day I discovered a gorgeous pair of riding boots in black patent with Swarovski crystals down the side. I loved them so much that I've also ordered them in baby pink leather and bright red crystal-studded patent too!

It's one of my pet hates to see a beautifully turned out horse with a scruffy rider wearing an un-ironed T-shirt tucked into a shabby old pair of jods. Fair enough, if you're mucking out stables you don't want to be wearing Louis Vuitton (although I do have a very nice padded Vuitton jacket that I wear to the yard) but when I go riding I like to look as groomed and coordinated as I do at all other times. So I've never really worn what people would consider conventional riding gear. Instead, I tend to ride in my own KP Equestrian stuff or normal clothes that I've already been photographed or filmed in, which means that I can't wear them again because the papers make a big deal about me wearing the same thing twice. In this picture, which was taken just after I'd come in from a morning out on my horse, I'm wearing a black and silver jumper that I wore for the launch of one of my perfumes and a diamante-studded T-shirt by one of my favourite brands, E.vil.

Hanging out at the stables with my ex Dane Bowers, friend Sally and sister Sophie

My riding skills have come in useful throughout my modelling career too

As well as riding horses, I've also done a few photoshoots with them too

*I've always
loved horses and
riding them keeps
me relaxed*

With my horse Jordan's Glamour Girl competing in my first ever dressage event

Having said that, I do adore the classic dressage look; the long tailored jacket, spotless jodhpurs and shiny traditional hat. When I was lucky enough to be asked to perform at the Horse of the Year show I customised my jacket with a bit of diamante, but that was only because it was for a showcase. If I was doing a dressage competition it would be one of those very rare occasions in my life where I would be happy to be wearing the same thing as everyone else – although I would of course wear a full face of make-up. It's still my ambition to make the Olympic dressage team, but realistically I'm not going to have time to prepare for the 2012 London games, so maybe I'll try for the one after. Watch this space…

Because I get photographed so often, I don't like to wear the same thing twice in public but I will wear things again to go riding

I don't always wear conventional riding gear at the stables…

…which is why I came up with this look for my KP Equestrian range

RUNNING

These days, I don't like any form of exercise apart from riding. I wouldn't mind getting into another competitive sport like tennis (Junior is currently having lessons and is a bit of a star – my Junior Andre Agassi!) but I hate working out and try to stay as far away from gyms as possible. I'm pretty happy with the way I look without lifting weights in a room full of sweaty people, and I have absolutely no interest in wasting my life on a rowing machine. The last time I went to the gym was in New York just a few weeks before we ran the London Marathon, but only because I needed to train and I couldn't go to Central Park because there were too many paparazzi around, so I did two hours on the hotel gym's treadmill instead. Ah yes, the Marathon. I'm really glad I did it because I raised a lot of money for Vision, a charity for visually impaired children like

If only I could have got away with a cute outfit like this for the marathon

Me and Danny on marathon day

a proper pair of running trainers that I had fitted at a specialist running shop in Brighton (my mum has run the Marathon before, so she told me where to go) with a pair of running socks, an industrial-strength sports bra which I had made to fit, baggy T-shirt and long running leggings. I wanted to wear the long tights because I thought it would make me run a bit faster, like when swimmers wear those all-in-one bodysuits and hats to limit resistance in the water.

Some people doubted whether I could finish the marathon and although the last few miles were a struggle thanks to my knee injury, the photo of Harvey on my T-shirt really kept me going and reminded me why I put myself through this torture in the first place. Thankfully I was lucky enough not to get any blisters or chafing during training or the race itself, although poor Pete was rubbed raw and got a nasty skin infection. But I was hobbling around for days after the race.

So have I been keeping with up the running since I finished the Marathon? What do you reckon! Mind you, after a few weeks rest, I was tempted to start running again.

Harvey and I'm proud of myself for completing the full twenty-six miles and making it across the finish line despite struggling with a knee injury, but beyond that it was a complete waste of time and had zero benefits. I hate running – and I hated what it did to my body. After all the hours of training I ended up looking like a bulked-up bloke. Before I started preparing for the Marathon I imagined I would run it in a cute little outfit, shorts and possibly even a crop top, but when I realised what was happening to my body I covered up. I'm not into wearing tight little things when I look like the Incredible Hulk. My legs got so muscly that I got through three pairs of riding boots and my skinny jeans no longer fit. I know some people like it, but the pumped-up gym bunny look is definitely not for me. So my running gear consisted of

Drama Queen

Whenever I do my book signings and personal appearances most of the fans who turn up are women and girls, but the second largest group is always gay men.

My gay friends tell me that I'm considered to be something of a gay icon, which is incredibly flattering because there aren't that many young British women I can think of who have earned that title – and because most of the gays I know have fantastic taste! I think the reason for my appeal is partly down to my glamorous and sexy image, but also because I'm a strong woman who has come from nothing and fought bloody hard to get where I am today, dealing with shitty relationships and personal traumas along the way. It's all about the drama, darlings – or so my gay friends tell me! In return, I love the whole larger-than-life camp glamour of the gay scene. I have posed for the cover of the gay magazine Attitude with my mate Phil Turner in a recreation of the legendary Vanity Fair cover shoot featuring Cindy Crawford and the lesbian singer k. d. lang, and when I had my album out a few years ago I went on a promotional tour of gay bars. I always love a gay bar because they usually play the sort of cheesy 1980s music I'm into, plus they're always packed with hot men. I've also performed at G-A-Y, the legendary London club night, where I sang 'A Whole New World' with Pete. While I was getting ready to go on stage I was feeling pretty awful as I was pregnant at the time and was trying to keep it secret, plus the dress I had wanted to wear didn't arrive in time so I ended up wearing something I hated. But the atmosphere in the club was electric; there was a full house and as soon as I came on everyone went crazy, which instantly made me feel like a superstar.

So for this chapter – which could also be called 'The Gay Man in Me' – I've been inspired by my gay fans to unleash my inner drag queen and go beyond my wildest, most extravagant fantasies to create something completely outrageous. I might have started my career as a glamour model, but it's very rare that I have the opportunity to let my imagination run crazy and experiment with the sort of extreme looks that are usually only found in editorial shoots for glossy fashion magazines and on designer catwalks, a side of the modelling industry I've never really been involved in. Hopefully these pictures will go to show that while I might not have the height to be a fashion model, I can certainly pull off a catwalk look. There's a really camp element to it too; I can just imagine the legendary American drag artist RuPaul wearing that blonde wig and pink sequinned gown.

I haven't had a stylist for these pictures; it's just been me and my gay mates Gary and Nick going crazy with a huge pile of wigs, theatrical costumes and make-up. I love the different looks we have put together and although it might not be a style that I'm usually associated with, I would definitely go out clubbing in some of these outfits – especially the short blonde wig. See, I told you I was a style chameleon!

A Posh look for me

I can't wait to wear this wig out clubbing

Cyber slut

*Amy Winehouse
meets Cruella Deville*

*I've never done anything
like this before*

Kinky afro

Scarlet fever

I loved pushing
the boundaries in
this shoot

I'm a Barbie girl

11

Hair and Make-up

When it comes to creating my look, the way I style my hair and apply my make-up is just as important as the clothes I wear – perhaps even more so. But while the way I dress hasn't really changed since I was 18, it has taken me years of experiments (some more successful than others) to work out which make-up looks and hairstyles suit me best.

Like all little girls, I used to love playing with my mum's make-up, nicking her blusher brush and rubbing it over my face until I was blotchy and orange. I remember the first time I tried wearing mascara I hated how long my eyelashes looked, which is weird because now I'll happily pile on as many pairs of false lashes as possible! But I first started taking a real interest in hair and make-up when I was about 15. I started dying my eyebrows and eyelashes jet-black and would wear bright red lipstick with black lip liner. Just like now, I was obsessed with smelling nice and would cover myself with Body Shop Fuzzy Peach and White Musk perfume oils, Charlie Red or Exclamation. My hair would always be scraped back in a tight bun which I would keep in place with loads of grips down each side and I would leave one strand of hair hanging down the front which I would coat with hairspray that I got from the 50p shop. Honestly, I didn't have a clue!

It wasn't until I started modelling and working with beauty industry professionals that I discovered how to make the best of my features, and finally left the black lip liner and hair scrunchies behind.

Me and Gary

Shopping in MAC

These days my usual look could best be described as very low maintenance. I rarely wear make-up during the day – apart from a bit of lip balm – and my hair is usually scraped back in a simple ponytail. Even if I know I'm going somewhere I might be photographed, say shopping in London or arriving at the airport, I usually can't be bothered to make any effort. But I still love piling on the slap and transforming my look with wigs and hairpieces for work and big nights out, and I'm lucky enough to have a top celebrity make-up artist, Gary Cockerill, and hairstylist Melodie Pope among my best mates, who are usually on hand to help out.

Over the years I have tried loads of different products but there are certain ones I always end up coming back to, which I know work brilliantly with my hair and colouring and always deliver fantastic results.

MY TOP 10 HAIR AND MAKE-UP ESSENTIALS... ♥ ☆

Tigi Catwalk Honey and Oatmeal shampoo and conditioner
The only products I've ever used to wash my hair, they repair damage and add shine.

Tigi Catwalk Curls Rock leave-in moisturiser
This leave-in conditioning cream works brilliantly as a straightening balm.

Tigi Bed Head Brunette Goddess shine spray
A quick spritz makes your hair fabulously glossy.

MAC foundation (Studio Fix NC43)
The best foundation I've used, it gives brilliant coverage and doesn't budge.

BeneFit Bad Gal Lash mascara
This has got a really big brush which gives a fabulous false-lash effect.

Dior brow pencil (dark brown)
I fill my eyebrows in with light strokes then brush the brows into place with the comb on the lid.

MAC bronzing powder
Brilliant for enhancing a tan without looking like you've been Tangoed.

MAC or Stila lip glosses
I go for shimmery nude shades which make the lips look fuller

MAC brushes
- Girls, it's all about the brushes. Spend a bit on these – a set of good brushes make it easier to achieve a professional make-up finish.

Vaseline
My all-time ultimate make-up essential. I use it on my lips and to groom my eyebrows if I'm not wearing any make-up.

HAIR

Until my late teens my hair looked pretty much as nature intended, which is chestnut brown and wildly curly, but when I started modelling I discovered straightening irons and since then have never gone back to my frizzy roots. Since becoming famous I've tried every other style under the sun, from bleach-blonde dreadlocks for my stint in the Australian jungle to jet-black waves – and all the colours in between.

I do admit that there have been a few disasters along the way. Around the time of my first pregnancy my hair was ruined by a very well-known celebrity hairdresser. I'd gone to see this guy at his posh west London salon and he'd taken one look at my beautiful long hair and said he wanted to completely transform me. It will be great, he promised, really glamorous and sophisticated. A couple of hours later I left the salon with a baseball cap hiding my new hideous Meg Ryan-style bob and the tears that were streaming down my face. The next day I got extensions fitted for the first time, but as my natural hair was so short I had all these bits sticking up, like when Britney Spears had them put in after shaving her head a few years ago. They were so cheap that the glue bonds were really obvious so I had all these little

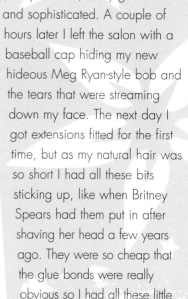

lumps showing around the hairline. Then I went through a stage of having all different coloured extensions put in, like baby pink and pastel lilac. Vile!

I can honestly say my hair's never looked better than it does today – and so it bloody should, the amount of money I've spent on it. I much prefer being dark to blonde, probably because I go lighter when I'm pregnant so associate being blonde with being fat and miserable. The darkest I've ever been is a glossy blue-black shade. To keep it looking its best, my friend Melodie colours it every three weeks using L'Oreal Richesse in Black, a semi-permanent colour

which gives a really glossy, healthy-looking finish. If I leave it any longer between touch-ups the roots start to show – and because my natural hair is so much lighter it looks grey against the black. Not a good look.

Growing out my disastrous 'do'.

My own hair is currently quite long, a few inches below my shoulders, but I feel naked without lots of thick, flowing extensions. I would love to have my hair cut in a really short pixie crop, just to see what it looks like, but every time I have the extensions taken out I'm like, 'Oh my god, I need my hair back!' It's like my security blanket! It also comes down to laziness, as I don't think I could be bothered to blow-dry and style my hair every day, which I would need to do with a shorter cut.

As I'm naturally curly I've always had to have human hair extensions, because you can't use straightening irons on the mono-fibre ones. The first time I had extensions it cost £300, but now I get them done in the States for a whopping $8,500 – and they only last a couple of months before I have to have them taken out and replaced, as my hair grows so quickly. The reason these particular extensions are so expensive is not just because of the quality of the hair, which women in India donate to temples, but the way they are attached, using a natural keratin bond which is barely visible. I know it's a crazy amount of money, but my hair is really important to my job, so I just see it as investing in my career! Plus, I can treat them exactly as if they were my own hair so it doesn't take me hours to style and care for them.

I know you hear horror stories about extensions making you go bald, but I have never suffered damage from them, even when I had the cheaper ones in. I think if you look after them and get them

removed professionally then they'll last longer and won't pull out your own hair.

As far as my hair care routine goes, I have it cut every time I have the extensions fitted as otherwise it can end up looking a bit witchy, and then Melodie will occasionally cut layers in when she colours it. Every time I have a shoot I get it washed with either my own Katie Price hair products or the Tigi range, which I have used for years, and professionally blow-dried straight. I don't think you should wash your hair every day, as it strips it of all the natural oils, so I probably have it done no more than twice a week. I bet you're thinking, Dirty bitch! If it is really greasy and I don't have work I will wash it myself and leave it, but then I'll have to wear it up as I hate it looking frizzy.

MY INSTANT BAD-HAIR-DAY FIX

1. Get a hairband and pull your hair through as if you were going to put it in a ponytail.
2. Instead of pulling the ends right through when you double up the band, pull if half way through and then secure with the band, so you're left with a bulge of hair.
3. Spray any wispy bits with hairspray to keep the sides looking sleek.
4. If all else fails, stick on a baseball cap. I used to wear them all the time, but I never do these days as I just don't think they suit me anymore.

My range of hair products

BLOW-DRY
STEP-BY-STEP

Step 1: Rough dry hair.

Step 2: Starting from the back of your hair, wind large sections around wide Velcro rollers and secure with a Kirby grip.

Step 3: Leave in rollers for as long as you can, until your hair is dry if possible.

Step 4: After removing the rollers, break up the curls using the hairdryer…

…and your fingers.

The finished look – body and texture

HAIRPIECES AND WIGS

I'm a huge fan of hairpieces, as they're an instant way to add volume and length to your own natural hair, and I've got boxes and boxes in all different shades and styles. They're also cheaper and more versatile than having hair extensions. I get all my hairpieces in America, as I find the ones you get in Britain just aren't thick enough so I end up having to use several to get the same fullness. But wherever you get them, I would recommend you always go for human hair rather than synthetic, as otherwise they can look really fake.

It takes a bit of practice to get a professional result, but the easiest way to use hairpieces is to create a sexy 1960s-style bouffant by putting your own hair into a ponytail and then fixing the piece

Even Harvey can't resisi trying on my wigs

using the attached comb and Kirby grips for extra security. The trick for making it look natural (apart from making sure you have a good colour match) is to leave a section of your own hair loose at the front, which you can then comb through the piece or over it – whatever you prefer. Also, never fix the hairpiece too close to your hairline as that will always look fake.

I only ever wear wigs if I want a complete colour change or I'm on a shoot, in which case I'll wear whatever they throw at me! Wigs are even easier to wear than pieces. First of all you need to hide your own hair. As my extensions are very thick, I take very small sections of my hair and wrap each section around my head, pinning with a Kirby grip as I go. Take them one way, then the other way, so your hair stays evenly flat to your head as you go round. If you're going to wear a short-haired wig it's always good to put a wig cap on top of this to stop any stray hairs from escaping at the back. It's not quite as important on a long-haired wig – you can get away with just pinning your hair up and fitting the wig on top.

I love a sixties-style bouffant

MAKE-UP

People seem to think I'm always caked in make-up, but unless I'm working or on a big night out I'll rarely wear it – and if I do it will be minimal. I don't even bother with tinted moisturiser; I think it's important to let your skin breathe. Anyway, every bloke I've ever been out with has said they prefer me without make-up. But I do always have my brows and lashes tinted so it gives my face a bit of definition, and it certainly helps that I've always got a tan. If you have a sun-kissed glow you can get away with it, but if I was pale and pasty I would be far more likely to wear make-up on a daily basis.

I didn't really work out what suited my face until I was 25 and to be honest I still can't do my make-up

TRICKS OF THE TRADE

⭐ For an instant wide-awake look I pull my hair into a tight, high ponytail to get a facelift effect, groom my eyebrows and stick on a pair of false lashes. I'm such a lash addict that I once tried individual eyelash extensions. They looked really good when I'd just had them done, but your mascara gets clogged in them and they pulled my own eyelashes out, so I'm sticking to my trusty MAC falsies. The most sets I've ever worn at once? Five!

⭐ To dress up your daytime make-up for evening outline the inner rim of the eye in a dark kohl. It makes the eyes really sexy. Or if I've had a heavy night and need to freshen up my eyes I do the same thing with a white pencil to make them sparkle.

⭐ Eyebrows are an essential part of my look and I feel all wrong if they're not in perfect shape. The more glamorous the look, the darker and more defined my brows will be.

⭐ What can you do if you get a spot? Panic! You could put concealer on it, but I'm not a big fan – you can still see the spot, it just looks like a crusty Rice Krispie. In emergencies, my mate Gary swears by a dab of toothpaste to dry spots out.

⭐ You'll never see me with matt lips. I'll always go for a glossy finish, as I think it looks younger and sexier, even if it's just a dab of Vaseline. I don't really like wearing strong colours on my mouth, unless I'm doing something like a 1950s pin-up themed shoot that requires strong red lips. I usually stick to glossy nude tones, which are the best for emphasising lips. For a plumper pout, outline with a lip liner, apply loads of gloss – it doesn't matter what colour – and blend with a lip brush.

⭐ People might think I'm caked in foundation but I really only use minimal amounts. I prefer my skin to be matt, as I don't like looking sweaty, but I'll often use an illuminator on my cheekbones to highlight and add shine.

Sexy eyes

I have loads of false eyelashes even ones with feathers on

properly. I'm OK at the natural look – a bit of foundation, blusher and Vaseline on my lips – but I still haven't got the hang of eye shadow. I find all that contouring, shading, blending and highlighting a bit confusing. Thank god my best mate Gary is usually around on the occasions when I want to pile on the slap.

But for someone who doesn't wear make-up that much, I certainly seem to have a lot of the stuff. I've only got a few items for daytime use, but when it comes to evening I haven't got a make-up bag – I've got a chest of drawers. I've got all different coloured glitters, lipsticks with matching liners, sparkly eye pencils, rainbow-coloured eye shadows… It's a make-up junkie's dream! Half the stuff hasn't even been used as I often buy things just because I love the packaging.

MAKE-UP MASTERCLASS – MY FOUR KEY LOOKS

NATURAL DAYTIME

This would be my typical daytime look: a completely naked face apart from perhaps a slick of lip balm and moisturiser. This picture was taken when I'd just come in from a morning's horse riding!

Eyes

Ensure your brows are perfectly plucked, brush them upwards to create a nice arch and then fill in any areas as necessary. To avoid a slug-like effect, make sure you use a pencil or eye shadow which is a shade lighter than your natural hair colour.

Sweep a single eye shadow colour over the lids and the lower lash line. I usually go for a nude skin-tone or a bronze with a bit of shimmer.

My lashes are naturally curly, but I suggest you curl your lashes for a wide-awake look, then apply one coat of black mascara.

Lips

Apply a clear gloss.

LUNCH WITH THE GIRLS

Skin

Apply minimal foundation to even the skin-tone and then dust over translucent powder to get rid of shine.

Use a powder bronzer to contour the cheekbones, then dust a little on your temples, end of the nose and your chin for a sun-kissed glow.

Brush a pink blush on the apples of the cheeks (the bit that sticks out when you smile) to add colour.

RED CARPET GLAMOUR
Skin

As before, apply foundation, powder and bronzer to contour, then add an apricot blush to lift the cheek. Avoid anything to rosy as this is a stronger, more structured look.

Eyes

The most flattering shades for green eyes like mine are ones with a bronzy, coppery tone, which really make my eyes pop.

To create this look, Gary used four different eye-shadow shades. Apply a mid-tone bronze on the lids, then on the outer edge of the lid and into the socket line use a deeper burgundy bronze to intensify the eye. Across the brow bone sweep a shimmery champagne shade, which gives a lovely soft look when blended, and then use a deep orangey-red shadow on the lash line and work it around the outer edge of the eye. A reddish-brown eyeliner around the inner rim of the eye really brings out the green in my eyes.

I love my eyes to have a sexy, feline look, so the most important thing here is to get the angle and shape of the eye right. Create a cat-like shape by drawing the shadow out to the far edge of the brow and angling it up at the end. Miaow!

Coat your lashes with black mascara, stick on a full set of MAC false lashes and then apply three more coats of mascara over the top, waiting between each coat for them to dry to avoid a spidery look.

The brows have been even more defined here to get that sexy Liz Taylor look.

Lips

Outline the lips with a beech-brown liner, taking the colour slightly inside the lips, then add lashings of nude-toned shimmer gloss and blend carefully.

JORDAN

Skin

The same products as before, just a bit more of them! You'll need a slightly heavier foundation – remembering to take it over the lips – and stronger contouring for this look. Use an illuminator on top of the cheekbones for a sexy sheen.

Eyes

Start by applying a coal-black matt eye shadow over the lids, the socket and around the eyes, then put a shimmery bronze-black shadow just on the lid so it doesn't look to chalky. A good tip is to dust loose translucent powder under the eyes before you start in case any of the shadow drops, then you can just use a brush to sweep it away once you've finished to avoid smudges. Use a light skin-toned shimmer powder on the brow bone and blend into the black.

Outline the eye, inside and out, with black kohl.

Apply black mascara, then three sets of lashes to each eye. I'm wearing two full sets on each eye, then I cut one in two and used each half on the outer edge of both eyes to make them look as big and cat-like as possible. Then pile on the mascara!

The brows are even darker, stronger and more arched than before.

Lips

Apply a natural-toned lip liner, then paint the lips with an iridescent silvery-white lipstick for a sexy Bardot-style lip. Finish with loads of clear lip gloss.

12

Beauty

I'm a complete beauty junkie. I must have tried every cream out there, from cheapo high-street basics through to top-of-the-range 'miracle' treatments. If you saw all the bottles and jars in my bathroom you'd be like, 'Holy shit, you should open a shop!' But I can promise you that nothing – and I mean nothing – beats wrinkles and freshens up your face like a little shot of Botox…

My daily skincare routine changes according to whatever products I'm using at any given time – and that tends to change on an almost weekly basis. I do start out with the best intentions though. I'll spot some new designer cream I fancy trying when I'm out shopping and will then get the entire range: the moisturiser, night cream, cleanser, toner, scrub, serum, mask, eye cream – the whole lot. I've tried all the expensive brands, from Crème de La Mer (which I didn't think was up to much) to La Prairie. I was even given a £1,500 crystal-studded jar of La Prairie caviar face cream, but I haven't used it because it stinks of fish. I like my skincare products to smell nice.

So for the first few days of using my new products I'll be really spot on, making sure I do all the different stages and carefully applying them with the correct massage techniques. But then one day I'll be in a rush, so I'll just slap on the moisturiser and skip the rest of the stages, and pretty soon the jars will have been opened a while and I'll have spotted something else I fancy trying, so I'll give up and move on. No wonder my bathroom is full of barely touched products.

I've always been lucky to have clear skin

I must admit I've been very lucky with my skin, although I do make an effort to look after it. I always make sure I cleanse and moisturise every morning and evening, and I would never go to bed with make-up on, no matter how knackered or drunk I was. Then once a week I go for Crystal Clear Microdermabrasion facials, where tiny crystals are used to blast away the top layer of dead skin cells. It's not a cheap treatment, but it gets rid of dull patches and fine lines brilliantly and it doesn't make you spotty like most facials seem to. I'm not actually prone to pimples, but I did get a breakout on my chin when I was in America recently so I went to see a dermatologist who suggested a mild chemical peel. Before she painted the glycolic acid onto my skin she warned me it might sting a bit – and she wasn't wrong. Oh my god, it burned like hell! The next day I had this hideous red rash on my chin, but two days later there wasn't a single spot left. I'll definitely be trying that again if I need to.

TANNING

Everyone looks better with a tan; well, I certainly do. Pale is definitely not interesting. So as much as I pamper my skin with facials and expensive creams, I also batter it on the sunbed. If you looked at my face through one of those machines that show up sun damage it would look absolutely diabolical because I've had regular sunbed treatments for as long as I can remember. We have one at home by the swimming pool and I'm on it pretty much every day, not only because I love having a natural-looking tan, but in chilly old Britain it really helps to warm me up too. Of course the risk of cancer worries me, but I hate being pale, and yes, I have tried fake tan but it's just not the same as a real one. I used it while I was pregnant with Junior, but the smell was disgusting, it came off in grubby brown smudges all over my sheets and the tan itself faded really quickly, so until they invent something that works better I'm afraid I'll be sticking with my sunbed. I look at it this way: I don't smoke, I rarely drink, I don't take drugs – my only bad habits are sunbeds and Botox. OK, so I'm probably damaging my skin, but I'm going to get old and wrinkly anyway so I might as well have a nice golden glow while I'm at it!

HAIR REMOVAL

Every time I have a bath, which is at least once a day, I shave my legs up to the knee, under my arms and my bits, plus I do my arms every week or so. I do this without fail so I've always got silky smooth skin. It's not that I'm particularly hairy, but there's nothing worse than being stubbly, especially on your bits. I'd hate to be a hairy hedgehog down there! In my opinion, there's no point wasting money on special ladies' razors: I've always used a basic man's Gilette disposable. I find it gives a far cleaner cut than anything else I've tried. I wouldn't bother with shaving foam either, I just use a bit of shampoo or soap to help the razor glide smoothly. People have asked how I can do my bits with a razor: well, to put it bluntly, it's called pulling the lips about! I usually sit on the edge of the bath and use a mirror so I can see what I'm doing, but to be honest I've been doing it so long I can pretty much do it by instinct. I'd never, ever have a Brazilian wax as I don't think I could stand the pain. I had my legs done once and that was bad enough; I've still got a long white scar down my leg from where they yanked the wax off a bit too hard. I am tempted to have the hair on my bits lasered off completely, as my friend's had it done and it looks brilliant, but again I'm too scared of the pain. Apparently it's like having elastic bands snapping against your skin. No bloody way!

I don't think you should ever get your eyebrows waxed either, as the skin round your eyes is so delicate. All that stretching and stripping encourages wrinkles, plus make-up never blends as well on waxed skin. I either have my brows professionally plucked or if I'm in America I have threading, which is really quick and gives fantastic results.

NAILS

OK, I admit it, I'm obsessed with getting my nails done. I have a manicure and pedicure at least three times a week by my nail technician Abbie, who comes to my house and will always match the colour of my varnish to my outfit. Even when I was running the London Marathon I made sure I had bright orange nails to match my T-shirt! I usually have acrylic nails, as I find they last longer than any other system and you don't have the same problem with chipping as you do with natural nails. Over the years I have tried every colour of varnish imaginable, but these are the brands and shades that I use the most often:

Essie (Short Shorts)

Essie (Shorty Pants)

Mulani (Breezy)

Orly (Lift the Veil)

Color Club (Lazer Pink)

OPI (Lincoln Park after Dark)

China Glaze (Ruby Pumps)

MY BEAUTY MUST-HAVES

Johnsons Baby Oil
I always pour loads of this in my bathwater, as I like my skin to be really oily when I get out. I hate having dry, flaky skin.

Dr Nick Lowe Spot Gel
I don't often get spots, but if I do get a breakout this stuff is genius at clearing them up. You can get it at Boots.

Champneys Bath Oil
I wish you could buy scented bath oils in big bottles: I love smellies and could easily use up a whole bottle in one bath.

MAC wipes
These can shift the heaviest of make-up. They are an absolute must, I love them.

Chanel eye make-up remover
This is the best eye make-up remover ever. It's not cheap, but is so effective.

Nivea Crème and Astral
When it comes to a good moisturiser, you really can't beat these old classics. They might be a bit greasy on some people, but I think they're great.

Decleor
I love their body treatment oils and creams, but I'm not so keen on their facial products.

Coco Chanel and Bijan
I've got hundreds of perfumes but these are the ones I'll always come back to, along with my own fragrances Stunning and Besotted.

Chocolate face masks from Superdrug
I love those really cheap little sachets of face masks. I'm not sure they do anything, but I like to do my little pampering bit when I'm in the bath.

Benefit bath hat
My hair has usually been blow-dried, so I protect it when I'm in the bath with a bath hat. This satiny pink one is among my favourites.

How my face has changed over the years

2009

EXTREME BEAUTY

Apart from wanting bigger boobs when I was a flat-chested teenager, I've always been pretty happy with the way I look. I'm not saying that I'm stunning, but I can get my get kit off for photos without needing to be airbrushed. So it's not like I need to have Botox or even that I hated my nose before I had surgery – in fact, I quite liked it. But I can afford to have these things done, and I like the way I look after having them, so why shouldn't I? I'm not doing it because I'm insecure with my looks or obsessed with surgery, whatever rubbish people accuse me of. I just don't think there's anything wrong in trying to achieve perfection. However, it is important to realise that it doesn't matter how many times you go under the knife, it will never change your life or the look in your eye. Some people make the mistake of thinking that breast implants will make them happier, but you'll still be the same person with the same problems, just with bigger boobs.

I haven't had half as much surgery as everyone seems to think anyway. At the last count it's five boob jobs and a nose job, plus veneers on my teeth, Lipo on my lips (which didn't work) Botox and injectable fillers. Despite the rumours, I've never had a facelift though. No bloody way! My mum had her face done years ago and I saw what she went through and how long it took her to recover. Anything from the neck down is fine as you can cover it up, but when it comes to your face you only need one fuck-up and that's it. Having said that, I'd have my eyes done if they get all baggy when I'm older. Oh, and I haven't had a 'designer vagina' operation either. I did have surgery down there, but it certainly wasn't to tighten things up or make it look prettier, as I'm perfectly happy with the way things are and nobody else has ever complained! It was because I suffered a prolapse after having Harvey and needed surgery to lift my womb. Glamorous, eh?

2008

2008

2009

My body shape has changed over the years too

2009

BOTOX AND FILLERS

As I said before, forget your fancy creams – Botox is by far the best thing I've found for making you look younger and more radiant. All it takes is a few quick jabs and then about five days later your face is transformed. Even though I hate needles I'm a massive fan, and everyone else I know who's tried Botox always goes back for more. Pete has had it too, but in my opinion it works better on women: I think blokes need a bit of character in their faces.

People are scared of Botox as they think their face is going to end up frozen and blank-looking, but I don't have a very expressive face anyway so I don't worry about not being able to show emotion. It's not like I'm an actor and need to have that ability. But I do think some people take it too far. I've heard you can get your whole face Botoxed, but I would never want that – just my forehead and around the eye area is fine.

I started having Botox injections just before I got pregnant with Junior and now I have it topped up every four months or so. I try and get it done in America, as they use a stronger product over there which lasts longer. It doesn't even hurt that much, it's more the sound that bothers me: every time the needle goes in it makes a weird clicking sound, almost like a stapler. But it's well worth any discomfort for the brilliant results.

Along with the Botox, I've been having injectable filler for about a year now. I love the effect, and unlike Botox the results are instant and last up to a year, but oh my god, it is so painful. I have it injected into my cheeks to give me a fuller-looking face, as I'm so slim that I can look a bit gaunt, but you can have it all over your face to fill in lines and add volume. I've had my lips done with filler a few times too, but I won't be trying that again. They didn't need doing in the first place and I ended up looking like Daffy Duck. Thank god they're almost back to normal.

NEEDLE KNOW-HOW

💜 You pay for what you get, so don't just go for the cheapest option. You can pay £150 to get Botox at a beauty salon by a visiting nurse, or go to a specialist clinic to see a doctor for double that. Even if I didn't have as much money, I still know which option I'd prefer.

💜 Botox only lasts a few months, so you should expect to need treatments every three to four months.

💜 You shouldn't bruise with Botox, but it's likely you will with fillers so if you're having it done for a special occasion be sure to schedule the appointment far enough in advance for any bruising to go down.

💜 You can get all different types of filler, e.g. Restylane, Juvederm and Sculptura. Any good clinic will be able advise you which is the best option for you.

💜 With filler your doctor may inject a local anaesthetic to numb the area beforehand, but not for Botox.

💜 Don't be afraid to ask questions. When it comes to injecting substances into your face you don't want to mess about.

TATTOOS

I think tattoos are addictive; I certainly want to have more. I've just got to work out what designs to go for and where on my body to have them done, because I'm running out of possible places! I'd never have them on my upper arm for instance, as that can look a bit butch.

I've currently got a bow on my back and a heart on my bits, which I had done years ago in Brighton just after I'd split up with Dane Bowers. It bloody killed, but even though I hate needles I don't mind tattoo needles too much. I think it must just be medical needles I object to! I've also got a bow with two hearts around my ankle, which I had done in Cyprus. That one was inspired by Nicole Ritchie's tattoo, which looks like a crucifix hanging around her ankle, and I wanted to have something similar, but the tattoo

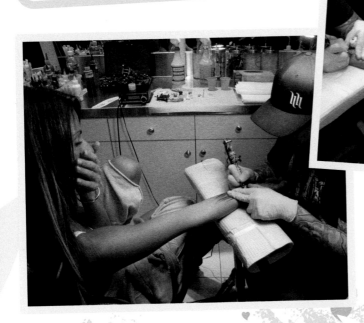

*My love
heart tattoo*

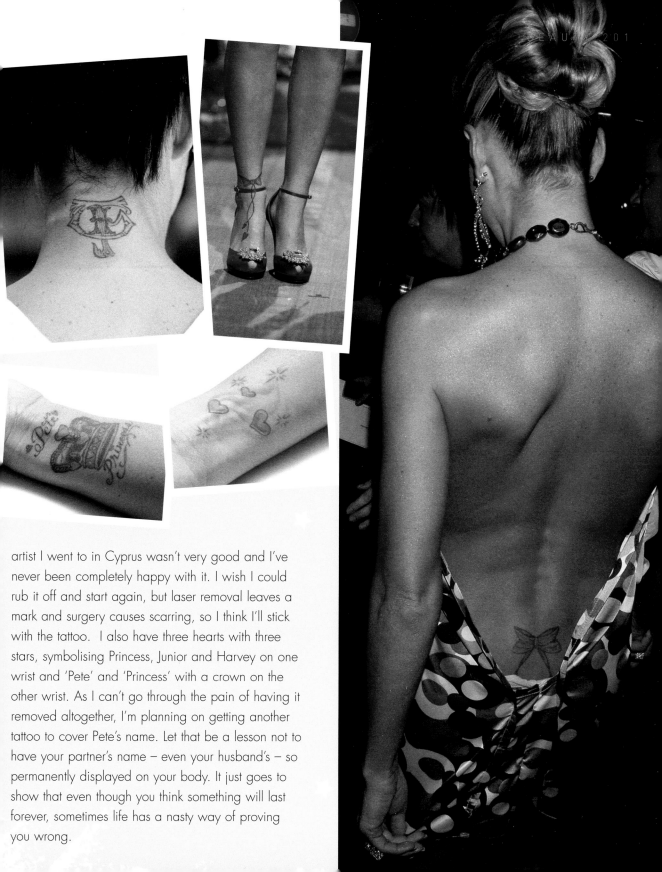

artist I went to in Cyprus wasn't very good and I've never been completely happy with it. I wish I could rub it off and start again, but laser removal leaves a mark and surgery causes scarring, so I think I'll stick with the tattoo. I also have three hearts with three stars, symbolising Princess, Junior and Harvey on one wrist and 'Pete' and 'Princess' with a crown on the other wrist. As I can't go through the pain of having it removed altogether, I'm planning on getting another tattoo to cover Pete's name. Let that be a lesson not to have your partner's name — even your husband's — so permanently displayed on your body. It just goes to show that even though you think something will last forever, sometimes life has a nasty way of proving you wrong.

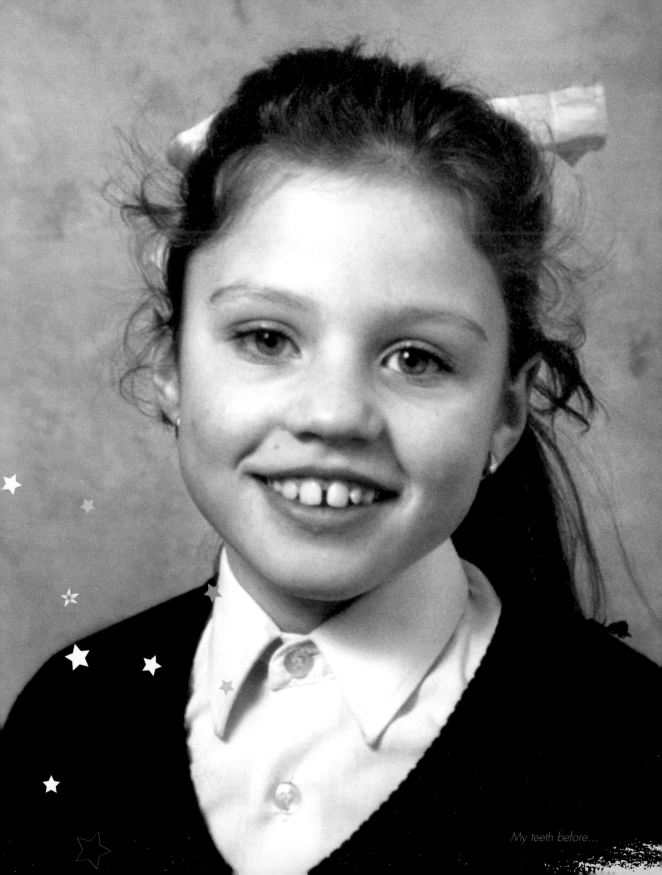

My teeth before...

TEETH

My teeth have always been an issue, ever since I fell off my brother's skateboard at the age of 7 and cracked one of the two front ones. The dentist put a cap on it, but the one next to it became discoloured and then they didn't match, so when I was 17 I got veneers (a very thin layer of porcelain which fits over each tooth) on my front six teeth to even out my smile. But like any sort of surgery veneers don't last for ever, so a couple of years ago I paid an extortionate amount of money to get them redone in America – and I have had problems with them ever since. For months afterwards it felt like electricity was shooting down my teeth, then the other day one of them fell out while I was eating a hamburger and now my bite isn't even.

So am I happy with my teeth now? Not really, no. I keep analysing them in the mirror and think they could do with being a bit straighter or a bit more even, but I'm not having anymore shit done to them. I've had enough.

...and after

NOSE

Whenever I've had my boobs done in the past I've always stood in front of the surgeon in my knickers and bra and asked them what else they'd change about me, and every single one of them has said they'd do my nose, so eventually I just decided to go ahead and do it. I wasn't unhappy with the way it looked before, although sometimes it looked a bit wide and cat-like in photos. Now it's neater and cuter, like a little fake ski-jump, but to be honest the change is pretty subtle. It's not like some people whose nose jobs really change the look of their face.

My nose before...

...and after

BOOBS

Once upon a time there was a little girl called Katie who dreamed of having big boobs. Then one magical day her wish finally came true! Katie loved her new boobs so much she would show them off at every opportunity. As the years went by they got bigger and bigger, until one day she looked in the mirror to see to her horror that her beautiful big boobs had turned into droopy big boobs. There was only one thing for it – Katie would have to get them made smaller again. And so she did, and she lived happily ever after… Except she didn't, did she? Five boob jobs later and I'm still not bloody happy.

It seems like everyone is having their boobs done these days. The press made such a huge deal about it when I first had my implants done all those years ago, but now it's so commonplace that changing your cup size seems no more shocking than changing your hair colour. But as with any major surgery, it's important that anyone considering implants asks themselves why they want to do it. If it's for a boyfriend or to look more attractive to men I'd strongly advise against it, but I can understand why women who've lost a lot of weight or who had babies want to replace what they had before. Personally, I just always liked the way bigger boobs look, even when I was at school, and I thought about it for years and did loads of research before finally going through with the operation.

If Princess comes to me when she's 16 asking to have a boob job I'll make her wait until she is 18, although after that she won't need my consent – and if she's anything like her mother she'll go ahead and do it anyway. But I'll make sure I talk to her about exactly why she wants surgery, help her to find the best surgeon and support her throughout the whole process.

So for the record, this is what I've actually had done. I started out as a 32B and after my first surgery went up to a 32C/D. When I saw them after the operation I thought, Oh my god, they're not big enough, and so a year later I had them boosted to a 32D. But to my disappointment they didn't look any different and I knew straight away I'd have to have them done again. The third operation took me to a 32DD and gave me a bit more uplift. Then after having babies my boobs got droopier and I realised I'd need to have them reduced. Even if you don't breastfeed your boobs really do change when you have kids; not only do they sag but you lose volume too. So what I had was an uplift, in which they cut the nipple off, squeeze the excess skin together and then sew the nipple back on. It leaves you with what's called an anchor scar, which goes around the nipple and then in a vertical line down the underside of your boob. My scar wasn't that bad and it doesn't bother me anyway – it's not like I'm going to do topless anymore. But the operation wasn't a success: because I had such big boobs they didn't take enough skin away and the implant was really moving around. I wanted them to look like bullets. So I had to go back again to get it corrected. Now they're definitely smaller, although I do still wear a DD cup.

So yeah, I've had five boob jobs, but I wouldn't have needed the second one if the surgeon had gone as big as I asked in the first place, and I only had the fifth one to correct the botched reduction. So really I've only had three. But yes, I will keep going back and getting them redone as necessary. If I have another four or five kids I'll definitely need to as they'll look gross!

HOW TO GET THE BEST OUT OF YOUR BOOB JOB

1. Shop around and do your research: never, ever go for the cheapest option. (Having said that I thought I was going to the best surgeon in Los Angeles for my boob reduction and they still fucked it up.)

2. When you speak to your surgeon, ask to see before and after pictures of their patients or even ask if you can talk to some of them.

3. If you're having implants the operation will usually take about an hour and a half and an overnight stay in hospital. You'll feel tired and sore for about three days afterwards and will need lots of painkillers and rest.

4. If you're going to pay all that money to get implants you'll want to look after them properly. You might be tempted to go bra-less, but gravity's going to be pulling them down so make sure they're well supported. I always sleep in a sports bra.

Before the many boob jobs

13

My Photoshoot Diary

've never been good at early starts. I would much rather start work a bit later in the morning and keep going into the evening to make up for it. Luckily we're doing the shoot for *Standing Out* at my house, so while the rest of the team has to get up early to arrive here for a 10am start, I can grab a precious few extra minutes in bed. Not that I ever get the chance to have much of a lie-in these days: like most mums my morning usually starts a good hour or two earlier than I'd ideally like it to!

I always say that my house is nothing like a normal home. With all the people milling around — friends dropping over, couriers delivering packages, the cleaners and gardener coming and going — it's more like a busy hotel. Sure enough, when I come down to the kitchen to get the kids their breakfast one of the nannies is already here and a plumber has just turned up to fix the central heating. I like to have the heating on at a tropical temperature at all times, even in the summer, so when it packed up yesterday it was an emergency situation! The TV is blaring out SpongeBob SquarePants cartoons at full volume while Princess sits at the table doing some colouring and Junior tries to persuade the nanny to get his new hamster out of the cage to play with. We keep telling him that the poor animal needs a bit of sleep, but he's hamster-obsessed at the moment. It's a typical morning's chaos, but to be honest I'm so used to it now that I think a bit of peace and quiet would freak me right out! Then my mum arrives to take Harvey to school. She also helps me with my fan mail, so while I grab

a bowl of cereal for breakfast I sign a few autographs for her to send off.

Once the kids have been packed off for the day I quickly get changed into my riding gear and jump in my car to drive to the stables. For me, an hour on my horse is the best way to start the day, but these days it's quite a luxury as I'm usually rushing off somewhere for work. Riding is one of the very few times in my life that I'm completely alone and have the chance to have a really good think. The combination of the

fresh country air, spring sunshine and exercise sets me up for the day ahead, and in the car I sing at the top of my voice to a Rihanna CD all the way home.

When I get back, the team have already arrived and are busy setting things up for the shoot. My friend Jamelah, who also works as my stylist, is unloading bags of designer clothes from her car and hanging them up on rails in our conservatory, which we're using as a dressing room. I can't resist having a nose around and spy some gorgeous Giuseppe

Zanotti heels – we're definitely using those for one of the shots! The shoot is taking place in our cinema room, where we usually watch DVDs on a huge pull-down screen. I'm planning on getting proper cinema-style seating and a popcorn machine, but for now it's easy just to push the leather sofas to one side so the photographer Andy has enough space to set up a temporary studio for our week-long shoot.

I haven't had a chance to get in the bath yet – let alone brush my hair or put on any make-up – when

Andy grabs me for a few photos of me with my 'natural' look. Yeah right, my 'sweaty-just-got-off-a-horse' look, more like! But I want this book to be about every aspect of my style, warts and all, so I strike a few poses in my jodhpurs and riding boots. I've been a model for years now and I know I'm good at what I do, so after a couple of minutes I say, 'I reckon you've got that now Andy, haven't you?' and he'll be like, 'Just a few more Kate!' Andy's great and we have a real laugh, but some

photographers I've worked with will snap away for hours and hours if you let them. I've been doing this long enough to know when the perfect shot's in the bag.

Someone sticks a cup of tea in my hand and I head upstairs for a bath. In my bedroom Gary has already laid out all his make-up. Every surface is covered with little pots, compacts and brushes and you can barely see my bed for all the crazy wigs and hair pieces that Nick (who creates my more extreme hairdos) has brought with him. Thank god Princess isn't here, or there would be glittery gold eyeshadow scattered all over my white bedroom carpet by now…

The first pictures we'd like to take today

are some step-by-step photos as I do my hair, so I wash it while in the bath, stick on my Juicy towelling robe and then my hair stylist, Melodie, starts putting my hair into rollers. While she gets to work, the whole team crowds into my bedroom and we flick through the style magazines and photographic books that Gary has brought with him to get some inspiration for the more creative looks we'll be doing later in the week. I've had this idea of doing a chapter called The Gay Man in Me (which we will later call Drama Queen) featuring really glamorous, drag-inspired make-up looks and huge wigs. Everyone gets excited about creating something extravagant, over the top and completely different from anything I've done before. I think we might have to add an extra day or two onto the shoot for everything I've got planned!

As Melodie does my hair, Andy takes photos of each step so we can recreate the whole styling process in the book. The pictures are taken in my bedroom so I don't have to keep on going up and down stairs, and the whole thing takes about an hour. Once my hair is styled, Gary steps in to do my make-up. Because we've got so many outfits to get through, we'll be starting with the more natural looks – like beachwear and mummy – and will then gradually build up the make-up to end the day with the really sexy, glamorous gear. While Gary works his magic I catch up with a few emails on my Blackberry and do a phone interview for my magazine column. It's typical really, I'm always doing three things at once! I'm told Kerry Katona has been talking about me in the press again, so the journalist asks me to comment on that and I chat a bit about the shoot, too.

Finally we're ready to start on the first outfit, which is for the Yummy Mummy chapter. I pick out a few tracksuits from the rails of clothes and then nip back upstairs to my own wardrobes to find the perfect matching accessories – a hairband decorated with cherries and black vest top. A few minutes of posing, then we check the photos on Andy's laptop – everyone chips in with their opinions – and it's onto a new outfit. Once we've got into the swing of it, things move fast and we easily get through six outfits in an hour, with just a few pauses to tweak hair and make-up. I wish all shoots were this easy…

By now it's about half two and the team is looking tired (lightweights!) so we break for lunch. The catering on shoots can often be rubbish – a few tired-looking ham sandwiches and some crisps is often the best you can expect – but today, we're in for a real treat, we've got barbecue chicken, potato wedges and cheesy spinach. Luckily my kitchen table can easily accommodate the whole team (plus my mum and little sister Sophie, who has just popped round) and as soon as the food hits the plates there is silence as everyone hungrily digs in. We have a bit of a debate about Lady GaGa whose latest video is playing in the background on music TV – it seems you either love her or think she's completely overrated (I'm with the latter) – but apart from that everyone is too busy polishing off the potato wedges to chat. As I reach for a third helping, I make a mental note to hold my tummy in extra tight for the afternoon's photos!

Then it's back upstairs for more make-up. This afternoon we're shooting the looks for the Sex Kitten chapter, which includes lingerie and kinky uniforms, so that means dark eyes, loads of lip gloss and huge hair – the sort of stuff I love.

This week's celebrity magazines have just been delivered, so as Gary sticks on my umpteenth set of false lashes we flick through and have a laugh at all the daft stories they've made up about me. Will I be 'dangerously skinny', or depressed about 'piling on the pounds' this week? Sometimes I've even been known to be both at the same time! I'm used to it now, but it can be a bit weird reading about this 'Jordan' character that the press have created. I mean, she looks exactly like me, but that's pretty much where the similarities end.

Time is ticking on; I've got to be in London to film an interview on Graham Norton's TV show this evening, so I grab another cup of tea and change into the first set of lingerie. When it comes to posing I prefer being pouty to smiley so I'm in my element with the skimpy, seductive looks we're doing this afternoon. Jordan's back folks!

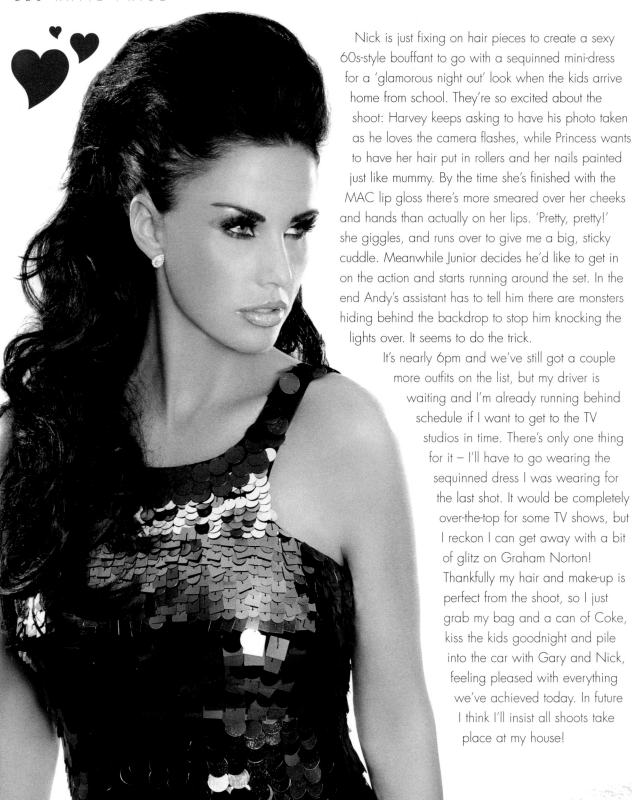

Nick is just fixing on hair pieces to create a sexy 60s-style bouffant to go with a sequinned mini-dress for a 'glamorous night out' look when the kids arrive home from school. They're so excited about the shoot: Harvey keeps asking to have his photo taken as he loves the camera flashes, while Princess wants to have her hair put in rollers and her nails painted just like mummy. By the time she's finished with the MAC lip gloss there's more smeared over her cheeks and hands than actually on her lips. 'Pretty, pretty!' she giggles, and runs over to give me a big, sticky cuddle. Meanwhile Junior decides he'd like to get in on the action and starts running around the set. In the end Andy's assistant has to tell him there are monsters hiding behind the backdrop to stop him knocking the lights over. It seems to do the trick.

It's nearly 6pm and we've still got a couple more outfits on the list, but my driver is waiting and I'm already running behind schedule if I want to get to the TV studios in time. There's only one thing for it – I'll have to go wearing the sequinned dress I was wearing for the last shot. It would be completely over-the-top for some TV shows, but I reckon I can get away with a bit of glitz on Graham Norton! Thankfully my hair and make-up is perfect from the shoot, so I just grab my bag and a can of Coke, kiss the kids goodnight and pile into the car with Gary and Nick, feeling pleased with everything we've achieved today. In future I think I'll insist all shoots take place at my house!

ACKNOWLEDGMENTS

A huge thank you to Gary Cockerill for being make-up genius and one of the reasons I'm always Standing Out; Andy Neal for never taking a bad photo – I do love a man who knows how to handle his long lens!; Nick Malenko for helping me release my inner drag queen, and for making sure she had fabulous hair at all times; Jamelah Asmar for being a style guru and all-round domestic goddess; Abbie Scott for changing my nail varnish over twenty times in one afternoon; Melodie Pope for keeping me sleek and fighting the frizz; Maggie Hanbury, as always, for her invaluable guidance and advice; Catherine Woods for all her help with this book; and Charlotte Haycock for helping make my vision a reality –
we got there in the end!

PHOTO CREDITS

With thanks to Rex Features, Getty Images, Press Association Images, Celebrity Pictures, Matrix Photos and Can Associates for supplying images for this book. Kind thanks also go to Danny Price for supplying personal photos. All other photography is Katie Price's own copyright.

STOCKISTS

JEWELLERY

Butler and Wilson
www.butlerandwilson.co.uk

Lola Rose
www.lolarose.co.uk
02073720777

SWIMWEAR

King's Road Sporting Club
www.krsc.co.uk
02075895418

Bikini Beach Star
www.bikinibeachstar.co.uk

CLOTHING

Doly by Dany Mizrachi
02074080010

Bernards of Esher
www.bernardesher.co.uk
01372464604

Club Esher
clubesher@yahoo.co.uk
01372469262

Styling by Jamelah Asmar
www.chicetmoi.com

Court Yard, Guildford
www.courtyarduk.co.uk
01483452825

Question Air, Wimbledon
www.question-air.com
02088790366

Pineapple
www.pineapple.uk.com

KP Equestrian
www.derbyhouse.co.uk/KatiePrice
0800 048 0114

Sequinned scarves by Alexia
www.alexiafashion.co.uk

SHOES

Giuseppe Zanotti
www.giuseppe-zanotti-design.com

UNDERWEAR

Katie Price lingerie range available in Asda,
Freemans and Littlewoods

Leg Avenue
www.legavenue.co.uk
08452702730

ALSO AVAILABLE
BY KATIE PRICE

NON-FICTION
Being Jordan
Jordan: A Whole New World
Jordan: Pushed to the Limit

FICTION
Angel
Crystal
Angel Uncovered
Sapphire

CHILDREN'S NON-FICTION
Katie Price's Perfect Ponies: My Pony Care Book

CHILDREN'S FICTION
Katie Price's Perfect Ponies
Fancy Dress Ponies
Here Comes the Bride
Little Treasures
Ponies to the Rescue
Pony Club Weekend
The New Best Friend
Pony in Disguise
Pony 'n' Pooch
Star Ponies

KATIE PRICE'S MERMAIDS AND PIRATES
Follow the Fish
Telescope Overboard
Time for a Picnic
Let's Play I Spy
A Sunny Day
Let's Build a Sandcastle